GOD IN THE RAINFOREST

by

Henry R. Loewen

authorHOUSE

1663 Liberty Drive, Suite 200
Bloomington, Indiana 47403
(800) 839-8640
www.authorhouse.com

First published by AuthorHouse 11/08/04

ISBN: 1-4184-6579-8 (sc)

Printed in the United States of America
Bloomington, Indiana

This book is printed on acid-free paper.

I dedicate this book

To my wife Edna
who lovingly walked with me

FORWARD

I owe the inspiration of this book to Jean Dye Johnson. She encouraged me in the beginning of our ministry among the Baniwa people. Later on she told me, "Your story must be written." I agreed, because it was Jesus' story, not mine. It took me some years to get all the material together. She coached and encouraged me.

After returning to Canada I began a radio ministry to the Baniwa people in Brazil, Colombia and Venezuela. Radio messages had to be prepared and sent to Trans World Radio station in Bonaire. This did not leave me much time to write. It took eight years to prepare weekly radio programs from Trevor McIlwain's book, BUILDING ON FIRM FOUNDATIONS. After that time we ran the programs the second time consequently I had more time to spend on this book.

Letters came from radio listeners asking me to put the radio messages on paper so they could use them to teach others. That was a challenge. Preparing the messages for the printer took a long time. It was much work. After that project finished I was able to spend more time on this book.

I received invaluable help from a dear person, who wishes to remain anonymous, to whom I am deeply indebted. Other friends chipped in to make the manuscript readable. Thank you, each one. A special thank you to Allan Bartel who kept my computer going.

The object of this book is not so much that my story be written, but that the readers know what the love of Jesus accomplished in the hearts and lives of the Baniwa people of the rainforest.

As I prepared the manuscript I was challenged over and over again. I could again feel the urgent the needs of the people in the rainforest. They had been waiting for a very long time to hear the message of salvation. Now they finally had it. They rejoiced in the spiritual freedom found in Jesus Christ. I was reminded again of the young fellow who told me he did not want to hear the Gospel story. His reasoning was that if he believed what the Gospel taught he would never get to see his deceased father whom he loved dearly. His father had never heard the Gospel. He wanted to go where his father went. He had not had the opportunity to hear. I wondered who had failed his generation.

When my faithful helper Joaquim heard me say that my father in Canada wrote letters to me, he asked me to send greetings to him. This started a friendship across the hemispheres. Both were thrilled to know they had the same faith.

It was marvellous to watch God work in the lives of hundreds of indigenous people of the rainforest. It was time well invested.

INTRODUCTION

As you read this book you will notice that our mission station had few buildings. There was a simple chapel where we gathered with the Indians who came to trade, and get medical treatment. This gave excellent opportunities to teach them the Word of God.

Joaquim, who was my helper for many years, lived on our station and taught often. Many times he asked me to teach. One time he mentioned that the Apostle Paul must have been an Indian, if not he probably was like Henry. What a compliment!

We taught the Indian children who came with their parents, to read and write. Our youngest two children went to the classes which Edna taught. Later on more workers who went from village to village to teach . This was difficult for the lady missionaries but they did a fantastic job!

Unfortunately, there were those who did not agree with the work we were doing. But, that is part of the story.

So, as you read please keep in mind that Jesus Christ was building His church among the Baniwa people living in the rainforest.

TABLE OF CONTENTS

CHAPTER ONE

ACCUSATIONS

An Indian runner emerged from the setting sun along the path into Sunset Village. He came to a panting halt directly in front of me and gave me an envelope. It had my name on it, in my wife's handwriting. At least she is fine, I thought; well enough to write a letter.

"When did my wife give you this letter?" I anxiously asked him.

"Ariki, she did not give it to me." He replied, using my Indian name. "Another runner gave it to me to take to you just two days ago."

"Did the other runner say anything about my family?" I enquired of him.

"No, he didn't tell me anything except that your wife told him to get the letter to you as fast as possible. I paddled as fast as I could and when I took to the trail I ran all the way."

"Thank you very much. Now I'll see what it says."

Nervously, I opened the green and yellow envelope. Would it be good news? Were the children sick? Why would Betty send me a letter with a runner? Was it sent simply because a passing traveler offered to take any message? God, you know what's in it. Please help me bear whatever it is. The first words I read said she and the girls were fine and I need not be anxious. What a relief!

Sunset Village

The agent of the Service for the Protection of the Indian (SPI) wanted me to meet him in Tunui Village, at the earliest possible date. She told him I had gone to spend time teaching the Indians and would find it difficult to leave them. The SPI had its headquarters in Rio de Janeiro and Inspectorates in every State that had resident Indians. Each local region had an agent representing it. Senhor Athayde Cardoso, the local SPI agent, told Betty it was very important for me to talk to him. He'd wait for me in the next village a short distance downstream from our station on the upper Isana River.

This was serious. I had just arrived at Sunset Village, to teach a week of Bible studies to the Curipaco believers. Four Indian church elders and I had traveled by dug-out canoe, powered by an outboard motor, for three days up to Snake Rapids. There we had left our canoe, chained the outboard motor to a tall tree in the jungles and continued on paddling in a borrowed dugout canoe. Finally we had arrived at Sunset Village and soon were settled in our hammocks for a rest before the evening meeting.

Almost two weeks earlier Betty, my wife, had wished me God speed as I left on this long trip to teach the Word of God to the spiritually hungry believers on the upper Isana River, near the Colombian border. Betty stayed at the station with our three daughters. They were well taken care of. Joaquim, my informant and his wife Dominga lived in a house next to ours. While Joaquim travelled with me, Dominga was happy to help Betty and our three girls. As usual when we left we committed ourselves and our families, to God's keeping, and then were on our way.

Betty and girls.

The Indians became very anxious when I told them the news in the letter. The old elder said, "We have waited for a very long time for someone to come and teach us more about God's Word. Must you leave us before you teach us even once? We have nobody to teach us from God's Word and we need you to teach us because we know so little." He continued to plead with me. What should we do? Should I ignore the summons and stay or should I go? After we prayed and asked God for wisdom, the church leader told me, "It would be better for you to go and obey the authorities as the Bible teaches us." During the meeting soon after sunset, God encouraged us and gave us peace. Everyone agreed I should return and meet the official, who was well known to most of them. We began our return trip down river in the light of the full moon. Strange feelings filled my heart. I was confident I was where God wanted me, I was certainly mystified by this turn of events.

Cooking meal on way to Sunset Village.

We paddle the last two days.

Sr. Athayde was surprised to see me so soon and wasted no time to tell me why he had called me. A letter of accusations had been sent to the SPI Inspector in Manaus who had, after much deliberation, asked the agent to check out the allegations.

"Henry," he said, looking at me. "I know you and I know what you teach. I have such confidence in you that I will dispense with normal procedures and let you read the letter yourself. Then I want you to tell me what actually happened in each of these charges."

There it was, a four-page document, signed and dated by a hostile religious leader from another mission. I was being accused of ordering the Indians to demolish the religious mission's chapels in several villages; teaching them not to use salt in their food, supposedly forcing very young girls to marry; and telling Christian Indians to poison those who didn't want to embrace the Gospel. He also accused me of training 400 Indian men with guns and rifles to drive the followers of the other religion off the Isana River. There were many other absurd charges. On the last page he appealed to the federal, state, military and civil authorities to help him to drive out the Evangelicals from the region.

While I was reading the document and denying the validity of each charge and explaining them one by one, Sr. Athayde was sitting in his small motor boat, taking notes. We had not ordered the Indians to demolish any chapels. Of course, we did not forbid them to use salt when, in fact, we always had salt on hand for them. We did not force very young girls to get married, neither did we tell them to poison those who didn't believe the Gospel. We were not training an army of 400 Indian men to drive the unbelievers off the Isana River.

When I had finished reading the charges against us and refuting them, he said, "Henry, I am well satisfied with your statements." He never again discussed this in any subsequent meetings. The issue, however, was not closed.

CHAPTER TWO

GROWING UP YEARS

I was born into a family that loved God. The Bible was prominent in our home. As I was the only son for many years my father doted on me. I was his boy. I can remember when I was still quite young, Dad would sit on the edge of my bed in the evening telling me Bible stories. A brother showed up in due time but I was still the oldest son. On the whole, we had a happy family life.

Sunday School for us was a rarity because the country church was too far away, especially in the winter. But we were well taught in the Bible and we all grew up trusting in God for salvation. Even before I gave my heart to God I was challenged to mission work. While attending an evening service where a missionary spoke about the great need of getting Bibles into Russia, my heart was greatly challenged. I decided that, someday, I would have a part in getting the Bible to unreached people.

I believe God honored my desire even though I hadn't given Him first place in my life. Conviction set in and one evening after hearing a message in the Gospel Tabernacle in town, I gave my heart to God. I hadn't yet had the opportunity to testify about my faith when one Sunday, some friends and cousins came to visit us, I shared my new found faith in God. My cousin told me later that because of my testimony he had decided to turn to Jesus. That was a real encouragement. When another cousin of mine heard I had been saved, she asked me to help her teach Sunday School in the local school. I argued that I had no experience and didn't know enough. That didn't stop her. She told me I had God and could learn from the lessons I would teach. I taught in that rural Sunday School until I left for Brazil seven years later in 1952.

Henry's Sunday School Class.

I loved farming, especially working in the fields. I took great pride in operating the sugar-beet equipment. In springtime I seeded our own fields and then the fields of nearby farmers. One summer day on my twentieth birthday, in 1947, I was working on the field near the road when Mother passed by in the family car with my fifteen-year-old sister waving good-bye. My sister was going to spend a week at Red Rock Bible Camp, open for its first summer camp. That was the last time I saw her. She drowned a few days later along with her counselor who attempted to rescue her. The whole family was devastated by her sudden death.

I continued to work on the farm, but felt the need of Bible training, so I enrolled in the Bible Institute in town about five miles from our farm. Classes in the Bible Institute began in early fall before the farm work was finished. I was determined to get as much Bible training as I could. After classes I was out on the tractor preparing the fields for the coming year. With the steady roar of the tractor in my ears I memorized many Bible portions. God was teaching me much about Himself.

Aerial view of Loewen farm.

God had things planned for me. A lovely girl in my class gave me a strange new feeling. We got to know one another and soon discovered we were meant for each other. Before I asked Betty to be my wife, I made sure she knew I planned to be a missionary some day. That suited her fine since she had the same ambition. We were married, put missions on the back burner and made great plans to farm with my Dad. God however had other plans. The following spring I rented a field to plant sugar beets. It was a perfect field, with the right kind of soil and no weed problems. Soon the tiny plants showed up in straight rows. It looked very promising. Then came a very hot, dry day with a strong south wind. As the wind increased, particles of moving soil cut into the tender shoots and soon many lay there wilting in the heat. When I saw this, I took the row crop cultivator to the field and stirred up the ground to stop the drifting soil between the rows. It worked but the wind had done its damage.

"God, why did you let this happen to me? What are you trying to teach me?" I argued with God, "I don't understand. I'll give all the profit from this field to you to use as you please if you permit it to recover." I was sure God listened to all this because later, the proceeds from that field were enough to take us through missionary training.

One Sunday we invited a missionary from Betty's church to have lunch with us. Susanne Plett, in her quiet way awakened the call to missions both of us had felt a few years before. Neither of us dreamed that seven years later we would bury her in the jungles of Brazil. The Holy Spirit impressed upon our hearts the need of giving the Gospel of Jesus Christ to the tribal people of South America. We prayed much about this and talked about it all the time. We couldn't get away from the challenge. I did not know then that my mother had given me to God for missionary work if only He would spare my life when I was very sick with encephalitis (sleeping sickness) at the age of seventeen.

My parents had a very difficult struggle with our decision to go into mission work, although mother quietly remembered the promise she had made. They loved God but also had plans for the farm and for us. God led us gently through those trying times. We found it hard to think we would be leaving dear ones behind. The Word of God comforted us when we read what Jesus told Peter after he boastfully told him they had left everything to follow him. Jesus answered and said, "Verily I say unto you, There is no man that hath left house, or brethren, or sisters, or father, or mother, or wife, or children, or lands, for my sake, and the gospel's, but he shall receive an hundredfold now in this time, houses, and brethren, and sisters, and mothers, and children, and lands, with persecutions; and in the world to come eternal life." Mark 10:29-30. We wanted to be faithful to God and serve him wherever he wanted us. Yet, it was hard to pull up roots and begin a very different life. God had promised never to leave us nor forsake us. Hebrews 13:5. So we encouraged each other and continued to look forward to serving God wherever he would lead us.

My father was an honest man and respected the wishes of other people, but now that it affected him so closely, he found it extremely hard to give in to God's direction for our lives.

One day after I had finished cleaning the hog barn, Dad walked in and said, "Henry, I want to talk to you. Henry, I've been thinking a lot about your going into mission work. I would like to buy the farm across the road and give it to you if you would change your mind." I had always encouraged him to annex that farm to his, and now he wanted to give it to me if only I would stay home and farm with him. That was a real temptation, but God helped me remain true to my commitment.

"Thank you, Dad, but I cannot go back on God's calling." He turned around and walked away with tears streaming down his face. Needless to say, it was extremely hard for both of us. He never again tried to persuade us to give up missions. From that time on he encouraged us to go and give God our best.

In a moment of weakness I told God I would go to the mission field for one term, and after that I'd join my father on the farm. That way I would satisfy my call to be a missionary and my desire to work with my Dad. Many years later, after Dad had passed away, several of his friends told me how hard it had been for him to have me leave him alone on the farm. They mentioned how they had tried to encourage him to stand with us in our ministry rather than to resist it. He gave in to God and became one of our first and best supporters. How I thank God for those faithful friends of his.

God blessed us with inner peace. We made application to New Tribes Mission and were accepted.

The day of departure came. We had the car all packed and were on our way to get the student permit from the American consul in Winnipeg. He objected strongly and wouldn't give us the required permit. Pleading was useless. I finally gave up and went down to the main floor of the building. Restless, I went outdoors and found a secluded corner and prayed to God for direction, while those waiting in the car had no idea of the battle I was fighting. God, I did not expect this to happen. Here I am, ready to go and the door has been shut. Please, dear God, show me what to do. After a while I sensed God telling me to go back to the immigration office and ask for the needed permit. "Okay, God," I said," It's your work and I'm your servant." I returned and a different officer waited on me who gave me the permit without any problem. Praise the Lord He had confirmed our commitment! We were on our way to the Missions Institute in California!

8

CHAPTER THREE

INTENSE TRAINING

Training was intense. The Word of God was taught from a missions point of view. There was much emphasis on dependence on the Word of God to be our guide. Bible classes began early every morning. Afternoons were spent in maintaining the whole campus. Every student was assigned to some work detail; and occasionally students would be asked to go to Mission Headquarters in Chico to help with maintenance. It was important for us to be able to work in harmony with others. Bad attitudes became evident and were dealt with. If we couldn't work with others in the homeland, how could we work with others in another country? We were encouraged to be open with others and share our burdens. We were being observed by the staff to see if we were growing in our faith. Weekends were spent in going out to nearby towns to share the Gospel with people there, either in their homes or on the streets. There was much instruction on how to establish indigenous New Testament churches. All this time God was preparing us for His work among tribal people.

The missionary training institute was located in a beautiful valley in the mountains within the Mendocino National Forest in California. The mission was using the buildings that had been used during the Depression to house men who worked in the forest. New buildings had been built for the use of the institute and for housing staff and students. There was an agreement with Forest Service that the missionary students would be on call to help fight forest fires whenever needed. This happened a number of times while we were there. It was in one of such fires that the mission lost nine men a few years later.

Strange circumstances took me through a deep valley. As a student at the training camp I was chosen to spend a few days at Mission Headquarters in Chico, California some fifty miles away to help with maintenance. My assignment was to mow the large lawns. This was no problem, but I struggled with the flower beds. I had never done that kind of work before; my mother and sisters took care of the flowers on the farm. On top of the problem with the flower beds I had a sore throat and fever. I felt so miserable

I stopped to lean on the hoe for a bit when the mission director passed by. He looked at me and said, "Henry, you don't look very productive." I was hurt by that remark. I had never been called lazy before. I was trying to do a job while feeling sick and feverish. I could have told him that I wasn't feeling well, but I didn't. Before long I went into the office building to drink some water and the director noticed me again. This time I told him that I wasn't feeling well. He gave me some lozenges and I went back to my work. The afternoon went by very slowly. When everyone else stopped working I did the same and went into the building where I met the director again. "Henry," he said tersely. "You may just as well go home today. The mission plane is going to leave for the training institute in a few minutes. Get ready and go along." The institute was located at Fouts Springs in a lovely valley in the mountains of the Mendocino National Forest. It would take a car several hours to drive that distance but the small Stinson plane could do it in less than half an hour.

I was anxious enough to return to my wife who was pregnant, but didn't appreciate the way I was told that I might as well return even before I was finished with my assignment. I was hurt. I nursed that hurt for quite some time.

Several weeks later we called for the same plane to take us to Chico, California, to the hospital, where Betty was to have the baby. The plane came and hurriedly we boarded, were buckled in, and were on our way. As the contractions came more frequently, the pilot pushed harder on the throttle to increase flying speed.

We landed and taxied to the ramp and there was the mission director. When I greeted him he declared, "You, again?" I was in no mood to reply but we gladly got into his car and in a few minutes we arrived at the hospital. Fifteen minutes later I was a proud father. Everything had gone fine and the next day we were at mission headquarters in a small apartment. After a few days we returned to the training institute by car to began life with little Audrey in our home. Classes continued for us. Since there was scheduled baby-sitting, Betty could attend most of the classes. The baby grew and so did the hurt in my heart. I was deeply disturbed that I had such bad feelings towards the mission director. I realized I couldn't go on this way.

Then one morning it was announced that the mission director would spend a week at the institute to give Biblical instructions relating to missionary service. That could prove to be an endless week. He gave classes for the whole week and then climaxed them by announcing we would celebrate Communion in the evening. How can I take Communion when I have these feelings in my heart? God, help me to straighten this out with the director, I prayed.

The classroom was empty now when the director came over to where I waited. "I must talk to you and clear my heart with you," I told him when we were both sitting down. He listened as I continued. "I know I am wrong in feeling the way I do towards you, and I want your forgiveness. It began when you talked to me at headquarters a few weeks ago. It was a hot day, I was feeling sick with a sore throat. When you passed by, you remarked that I didn't look too productive. The same day in the evening you told me I might as well return to the missionary training institute since the small mission plane would be going that way." I felt rejected and hurt.

"I discussed this with my wife and we both felt I should talk this over with you and ask your forgiveness. Then when it was time to take Betty to the hospital in Chico to have the baby we called for the small mission plane to take her there. On arrival you were there to meet us and take us to the hospital. When you saw me, you said, "'You, again?'" I was quite disturbed."

"I'm sorry I have these feelings towards you and ask you to forgive me. I can't freely participate in the Communion nurturing these feelings in my heart."

"You know, Henry, these are the very things God has been trying to teach me. I am sorry I treated you that way, please forgive me."

We both got up and embraced each other. The torment rolled off my heart that moment. We talked for a while about the unspeakable grace of the Lord Jesus Christ and His forbearance with His children. Communion had a special meaning for me that evening which I will never forget. The fellowship which had been restored was better than ever. Some years later the same director paid us a visit at our mission station in Brazil and was a real source of encouragement to us.

Several times during the missionary training course different groups would go into the mountains for jungle training. The group I was with took a wrong trail and the five-day hike turned into a seven-day hike. The institute owned a bus converted into a camper for students to go out and evangelize in various towns. I was never chosen to go on one of these two-week-long assignments of giving out Gospel tracts and telling people the Gospel fo Jesus Christ. However, Betty was chosen to go with a small group of ladies while I remained at home with little two-month-old Audrey. We all weathered these assignments and learned a lot.

The year went by quite fast. It was the end of the training, but we felt quite unprepared. The mission, however, accepted us as missionaries to Brazil.

There was much scepticism about our going to the mission field in our home area. Mission work was new to our church and there was no interest in supporting us financially. In fact, there was considerable opposition to it. I asked the church leaders if they weren't interested in standing with us in our ministry, would they permit us to join another church. That was preposterous. They wouldn't hear of it. There was no support forthcoming but we continued our preparation to go to Brazil. That last evening at home with our parents, three ministers from the church showed up and begged us not to go to Brazil with New Tribes Mission. They would support us financially if we'd agree to go to Mexico under the church's direction. It was too late. We were ready to go.

Dad's brand new Ford was packed the last day of 1951 and ready to leave the next morning. It was marvelous to see how God gave all of us such inner peace. My Dad and my father-in-law had decided to drive us down to Mobile, Alabama, where we were to board the *MV TRIBESMAN*, a ship owned by New Tribes Mission.

The car was packed to capacity. Audrey, by now 18 months old, enjoyed it all very much. Snow was piled high on both sides of the road as in a ravine. We were on our way!

We had no problem at the USA/Canada border as we journeyed south on that cold New Year's Day. Before long Audrey became feverish and sick. We gave her the regular treatment of aspirin but the fever didn't leave. That night, in our hotel room, Betty and I knelt beside our feverish daughter, anointed her with oil, asking God to honor His Word and heal her. Within a few minutes her body temperature was down to normal. We all slept well after that and started the next day with renewed anticipation.

By mid afternoon Audrey's small body was burning with fever again and aspirin didn't bring it down. That evening we stayed with a friend of Betty's father who referred us to a doctor. He gave Audrey an injection of penicillin for her sore throat. Her recovery was another way in which God confirmed our commitment.

CHAPTER FOUR - 1952

ON TO BRAZIL

We set sail to Brazil on the *MV TRIBESMAN,* a submarine chaser which had been converted to a passenger ship. It was owned by New Tribes Mission and was anchored in Mobile, Alabama. When we arrived we were informed the sailing date had been postponed, so we boarded and waited on the boat.

Days went by. Then weeks turned into a month and we became considerably anxious because the due date of the birth of our second child was fast approaching. For the time being, though, things looked all right and we simply trusted ourselves to God's leading. There were other ladies expecting to have their babies in Brazil. So Betty and I were not overly concerned about the delay in leaving. Really, it wouldn't be so bad to have a child born en route to Brazil, but we wondered what the little one's citizenship would be.

While we waited, we had the opportunity to purchase an aluminum boat and a motor to help us in our future ministry in Brazil. During this time our entry visas to Brazil had expired and we had to make new applications. The departure date was fast approaching and our visas had not arrived. God, however, worked and the new visas arrived just in time to begin the journey across the Caribbean Sea into the Atlantic Ocean.

The sea was fairly smooth but the swells were high and consistently rolled the boat from side to side. This was hard for us landlubbers and many were forced to rush to the railing to relieve their churning stomachs. Others just remained in their bunks nursing their nausea. Betty was one of those who, in her condition, remained in bed. That left me to take care of Audrey. We spent much time together on the deck watching the flying fish skid to a stop on the deck. She really enjoyed it. Being occupied with each other may have kept the sea-sickness away. Early in the mornings when all passengers prepared for breakfast, the crew played *He Giveth More Grace* over the loud speaker in rhythm with the rolling ship. The song made a deep impression in my heart and mind. Even years later, whenever I heard that tune, I needed to hang on to something solid because I got the sensation of a rolling ship.

As we were nearing South America, the captain of the ship announced that at a certain hour we would cross the equator. In the evening when the first mate read the sextant he discovered he had made an error the evening before. We were still north of the equator! That meant we would have the thrill of crossing the equator twice! Not only that, the first-mate's error placed us farther away from land than we really were, so we sailed over some shallow water where the mighty Amazon has been depositing silt for millenniums. The water was shallow and the tide was going down, so the captain ordered the anchor to be dropped. As a result the boat had an unusual rocking motion all night long.

In the morning new sextant readings were made, and soon we were on our way to the mouth of the Amazon. This was no small river! It is over 90 miles wide at the mouth with a 4,000 mile long body to give it enough volume to spew between 3 and 7 million cubic feet of water per second. This water is drained from nearly half of the South American continent as a result of an annual rainfall of over one hundred inches. The ocean tide reaches over four hundred miles inland.

We stopped to take on a pilot to guide the ship to the port of Belem. There were miles and miles of beaches on the coast. Farther into the mouth we saw small settlements with sailboats lining the sea-side ports. Then around another bend we saw a large two-story colonial building right in the center of a fair-sized town near the water's edge. The name of the town was Icoaraci. Within a few days we moved into that two storied mansion for the duration of the Portuguese language course.

Language learning was a challenge to us. It was very difficult to be in a country where we couldn't speak the language. God helped us to learn the language quickly; and after some months we were able to communicate with the people.

Joanne made an early appearance during a Portuguese class one day. We had previously decided, together with the doctor, that it would be a home birth. Soon the missionary nurses, living in the same house, had the excitement of delivering this bundle of joy into this world.

Everything went well during and after the delivery and we praised God for little black-haired, brown-eyed Joanne. Another missionary lady also waiting for her baby to arrive, saw how easy it had been for Betty and decided to have her baby at home too. But, two weeks later, things did not work out as well for Naomi and she nearly lost her life. The doctor arrived just in time to save her. Little Peter was fine but Naomi had to be hospitalized for some time before she recovered completely.

It wasn't long after Joanne was born that Audrey caught a severe case of impetigo and we were afraid Joanne would get it too. We had to be extremely careful about any contact between the two. It was difficult to keep Audrey from touching her new sister. The doctor who took care of Betty also treated Audrey's skin condition. I took her to the city of Belem by bus several times a week to see him. It was a learning experience not knowing the language and having a cute blond-haired girl with purple gentian violet spots all over her body. Everybody wanted to talk with us but we were unable to answer intelligently. This drove me to apply myself even more to language study.

As the months went by we were able to communicate more with the people and even give brief testimonies. Finally the time came when we finished the prescribed course and it was time to move on into areas where we would have a ministry.

We had come to Brazil to work with tribal people but when we finished the language course, the doors to tribal work closed. There had been some difficulties between evangelical missions and the Society for the Protection of the Indian - SPI, so we were unable to go into a tribe after finishing the language study. Carl Taylor, our mission director, encouraged us and others to go to any small town and begin evangelizing there until the doors to tribal work would open.

Al and Betty Hoenshell with their three girls were our co-workers, so together we prayed for God's direction and went to a small town called Peixe, situated on the Tocantins River, several hundred miles north of present-day Brasilia. To get there we had to get on an amphibious plane and go to Pedro Afonso, a cattle town near our destination. That plane made several flights a week to pick up a load of fresh meat for the city of Belem. When we got to Pedro Afonso we discovered there was no way to get to the town of Peixe, which was several days upriver, until the river rose high enough to go over the rapids, or until the road was dry enough to travel by truck. That could take six months.

We had no choice but to wait. The owner of an available house wanted two months' rent in advance. We paid it, but it reduced our cash to almost nothing. We expected our mission allowance to arrive the following week so it sounded feasible. The allowances, however, did not come. Week after week we met the mail plane only to be disappointed each time. We were beginning to be pressed for food. During this time a chicken strayed into our backyard looking for food. It even uprooted a lone straggling tomato plant. Nobody claimed to own the chicken, so our landlord told us to cook it for ourselves. That chicken with the last of our rice was so good!

The day after we finished off the chicken broth the former renter came to claim the chicken! What a predicament! God, what shall we do? I prayed desperately.

"Senhor," I said in my broken Portuguese. "We killed and ate your chicken yesterday. We didn't know it was yours."

He looked at me dumbfounded and replied after some hesitation. "Then you must pay me for the chicken."

"All right, we'll pay you for it. Can you come back tomorrow for the money?"

That still didn't solve our problem. We had no money and we couldn't return the chicken. We committed the problem to God, asking Him to give us wisdom.

The next morning Al, our co-worker, received a ten dollar bill in the mail which he quickly traded for Brazilian currency. That was more than enough to pay for the chicken. Thank you Lord! Al shared the rest of the money with my family, and it tided us over a few days.

We had been in Pedro Afonso several weeks when Audrey came down with a very bad case of diarrhea. In spite of all the medicine the local store keeper provided, we thought we would lose her All the praying we did seemed to no avail. She just got worse. On Sunday morning I picked her up, covered her with a thin blanket and walked through the town square, carrying her in my arms. Presently a woman walked towards me. With concern she asked me, "Is your child sick?"

"Yes, senhora, she is very sick," I told her. "She's had diarrhea for almost a week now and she's very weak."

"My husband is the town's doctor," she informed me, "but, he is away. However, I know what he gives to children with diarrhea." She gave me the name of a medicine and went on her way. I quickly went to the drugstore. "Please, open the store so I can get the medicine the doctor's wife recommended."

He immediately obliged. Brazilians love children and will do anything to help them. After the first dose Audrey began to recover. God had come through again. This was another confirmation that He was leading us.

That year the river never rose enough to take us to the town of Peixe by boat. We ended up waiting for the rains to stop so we could go by truck. When the roads finally were passable we sent our wives and children by plane on to Vianopolis, our mission's headquarters, while Al and I accompanied our belongings on a truck to Peixe.

We had quite a time sitting on top of the canvas-covered load of rice as we made our way along the winding roads through the dense forest, dodging numberless branches. There were several other men on top of the load as well as a full-grown live tapir. Tapirs are nocturnal animals, and this one wasn't used to riding on top of load of rice. Its feet were tied together with leader ropes and had to be watched so it wouldn't come loose and fall off. Tapirs live in the forest regions of South America. They look much like pigs. Their keen sense of smell and hearing warn them of danger. They would rather run than fight. Natives hunt tapirs for their meat and thick hides.

We forded several streams along the way. After having driven all night we stopped at a shallow place in the river for breakfast. The driver told us we'd have fresh fish for breakfast. We wondered how long it would take. In a few minutes he had tied together several sticks of dynamite, lit the fuse and threw it into the shallow river, and immediately the fish floated on the surface. There was our breakfast!

We finally arrived in Peixe and unloaded our belongings. We continued on to Anapolis which was the truck's final destination. From there we went by train to Vianopolis a two-hour ride, which was where we finally met our families.

After some weeks it was time to go to the city of Anapolis to be near the British mission hospital for the birth of our third child. Anapolis is a beautiful city located on the high plateau of central Brazil. The climate there is moderate. The city is the supply and trade center for the lowlands. A British Mission established a hospital there when it was still a small town. Arlene was born in this beautiful, plateau city of Anapolis.

To our disappointment our field leaders reassigned Al and Betty Hoenshell, our co-workers, to a different location, so we went on to start our ministry in Peixe by ourselves.

Right from the beginning there was a lot of opposition to the preaching of the Gospel. One morning we found all the Gospel tracts and pamphlets we had handed out lying on the ground in front of our house. There were, however, those who listened. An elderly widow and her married daughter had been the only believers in the town for many years. The daughter was a school teacher and offered to help me improve my Portuguese. I owe her a lot for her untiring help. She had wanted to start a small Christian school and now asked me to help her. The local people were very glad for the school, which they called "escola batista," a Baptist school. The townspeople had more confidence in a Christian school than in their own, even though they had no use for evangelicals.

Door to door evangelizing was beginning to bear fruit and people gained more confidence in us. Then I had occasion to go to the next town by plane. The man who had been most vehement against the Gospel asked me to deliver an envelope of money to somebody. Astonished at this I asked him, "Senhor Francisco, why do you want me, a foreigner, to deliver this large sum of money when your own son-in-law is the postmaster here?"

"That, Senhor Henrique, is the reason," he replied without hesitation, recalling the many times money had disappeared from the post office. The people, in general, had more confidence in "crentes," (as they called believers) than in their own people.

At the mission's annual conference in Goiania I was asked to consider going to work with the Baniwa people on the Isana River in the northwest corner of Brazil, now that the door to tribal work was open again.

Was God really leading us there? After much prayer and discussion Betty and I agreed to venture out to the area in the State of Amazonas to which our mission leaders were directing us.

The people in Peixe did not take kindly to this change in our plans. Even the mayor was opposed to our leaving. He asked for the address of our mission director and sent him a petition with over seventy signatures requesting we stay in Peixe. I explained to him, "We are under the field committee's authority and we will abide by their decision. If they permit us to stay then we'll stay; if not, then we'll go on to the State of Amazonas."

We waited for word to come from our field director. Week after week we checked the mail as soon as the plane dropped off the mailbag. After several months went by with no answer I approached the mayor. "Mr. Mayor, if in three weeks there is no answer we will be leaving."

"That sounds fair enough. I understand," he replied.

The three weeks went by and there was no letter from our field director. We began to pack what we would dispatch by boat to Belem. There was no other way to send our belongings since all rivers ended up in Belem, which is at the mouth of the Amazon River. Airplanes followed the same route. We boarded the next plane for Belem from where we would continue on to our final destination.

While we were waiting in Belem for a river boat to take our baggage and equipment to Manaus, we received the letter from our field director informing us we could remain in Peixe! What were we to do now? We were halfway to our new place of assignment, and we got word that we could have stayed in Peixe. Again we prayed to God for direction and felt we should continue on to the tribe.

Betty and our three daughters went on to Manaus by plane with Bob and Naomi Rich and their family, who had been assigned to the same tribe. I remained in Belem to accompany all of our baggage on the next river boat. While my family arrived in two hours, it took me thirteen days to get there on the wood-burning steam boat.

CHAPTER FIVE

UP THE AMAZON

We looked forward with excitement to working on the Isana River with Bob and Naomi Rich. To my surprise I found he had already been recruited to be the mission's supply man in Manaus. Bob was there to meet me when the river boat finally docked in Manaus.

The trip on the Amazon River to Manaus had proved very interesting. Every one wanted to know what a foreigner was doing on the slow moving, wood-burning river steamer. That gave me many opportunities to tell them of my faith in Jesus and that I was on my way to work with Indians on the upper Negro River. One man told me he had been working for the boundary commission when they demarcated the border between Colombia and Brazil. He took keen pleasure in telling me that he, and others, had to walk long distances in swamps crawling with alligators in the same region where we were going to work!

The sailors eagerly told me of a group of Irish missionaries who had made the trip on this steamer a few months previously, going up the Amazon River. They had, apparently, been quite apprehensive about sanitary conditions on board and had arranged to prepare their own meals in their cabins with a small kerosene stove. They boiled all their drinking water and ate no raw vegetables or fruits. The sailors finished the story by telling me a young woman of the group had died on the next leg of their trip, before they ever reached their destination.

That river boat did not have sufficient refrigeration on board to store fresh meat for all the passengers and crew for the two week trip, therefore the lower deck was converted into a corral for a small herd of cattle. One animal was used each day to provide fresh meat for crew and passengers. When cattle feed ran out the boat was stopped alongside some large floating island of grass. The deck hands would get into small canoes and with long machetes cut enough grass for the day.

The steam engine needed firewood which was picked up at predetermined points – sometimes during the day, but mostly at night. Wherever the boat pulled into port, men and women came running to the riverbank to relay the short logs to the boat. One sailor counted the pieces of wood in order to pay them accordingly. This extra income helped the people who eked out an existence, living in houses built on stilts, along the banks of the Amazon River.

The banks of the Amazon were low with no high ground nearby. When the boat arrived at the confluence of the Amazon and Negro Rivers you could see high red banks in the distance. Then suddenly we were sailing up the Negro River in black water instead of the white murky waters of the Amazon. We finally arrived in Manaus which is at the mouth of the Negro River.

A trader in Manaus was preparing to make a trip up the Negro River within a few days of my arrival. Since that was the only way to get our supplies to the Isana River, I was on my way again all too soon. Betty and the three girls stayed in an apartment next door to Bob and Naomi Rich. Departure from the busy port in Manaus usually took place after sunset. After the prevailing winds died down, it became safer to cross the wide bay on which the city was located.

I found there were maybe a dozen passengers on board the river boat, one being German and another American. Then there was one fellow who thought he had to be drunk to enjoy the long trip. Early, the first morning this man, in a drunken stupor, asked me where I was going. "I am going all the way up the Negro River and then up to the Isana River where I will teach the Indians about God."

"Oh yes," he slurred. "I know those people up there. I have been there to spray their houses with DDT to kill cockroaches and mosquitoes." Struggling for more words, he told me, "Those people up there sing. They used to be notorious scoundrels, now they work."

"What happened to them?"

"Well, a woman from Colombia went there to teach them the Bible. Now they are different."

This reminded me that the Apostle Paul told the Thessalonian Christians their faith in God had become known everywhere. Here I was, almost one thousand miles away from the Baniwa people, and I heard about their faith in God as a result of Sophie Muller's ministry. Those were the people I was going to work with. Lord, I prayed, help me to be an effective servant among the Baniwas.

The German and the American had been in Brazil for a long time. They had married local women and had families. Both of them were very critical of everything. Nothing met with their approval aboard the river boat. They vehemently criticized the food. Since they spoke English I spent much time with them trying to convince them that God, in whom they did not believe, loved them and wanted to give them eternal life. The captain, the cook and the deck hands considered me to be like the other two foreigners

20

and showed it when they killed a large turtle and served everybody except the three of us. We got only the standard rice and beans. But later on, the captain's wife seeing me sitting by myself reading a book, came up to me with a small covered dish of special turtle tidbits. Handing it to me she said, "I notice that you are different from the other two foreigners. You do not criticize our food, and I want you to have this dish of turtle, but please, don't tell them nor give them any of it." I was glad to be counted one of the nationals. I had never eaten turtle before, but found it quite tasty.

I was raised on the Canadian prairies and consequently had very little experience on water. I had learned to swim in the neighborhood swimming hole. I had some experience on the river during our time in language study near the mouth of the Amazon River, but I had never gone through any rapids before.

The last day of the trip took us through dozens of rapids. Apparently they were safe enough, especially for large boats the size of ours. Everyone else seemed to be enjoying the turbulent waters but I didn't feel safe at all. The boat rocked from side to side as the river pilot pointed its bow into the swift waters next to rocks obstructing its course. Senhor Graciliano, the owner of the boat and local merchant, was sitting in his easy chair on the open deck, obviously enjoying it all. He may even have enjoyed seeing me so nervous. Senhor Graciliano was a kindhearted man and assured me all was well. After we arrived in the small town of Uaupes he asked his son, Augusto, to give me a place to sleep in one of their warehouses. After a few days, he was to take me farther up the Negro River to the mouth of the Isana River. It took Augusto several days to get his boat ready to make the last lap of the trip. There I was in this small town known to be a religious stronghold. Its religious leaders had ruled this place for many decades and, apparently, intended to continue to do so.

The delay at Uaupes dragged on many days. I continued to sleep in the warehouse. Senhor Graciliano and his son Augusto had me over for meals. One day Senhor Augusto invited me to accompany him to his small cattle ranch. He had a number of Indian men working for him, keeping the weeds down and fences up. That day, however, he had another project for them. He told them what to do, in their language which he spoke fluently, and then he sat down in the open barn. "Senhor Henrique," he told me. "Never work alongside an Indian. If you do he won't work. Just give him his orders and watch him work." I made a mental note of that to find out, later on when living with the Baniwa people, if it really was true.

Finally everything was ready and Augusto told me to get my things together and put them in his boat. The trip normally took him eight hours, he told me. Again, we wound our way, in a much smaller boat, among huge rocks and boulders through the turbulent waters. The boat rocked back and forth; many times the swift current swept it backwards. This was all very scary to me. I had to tell myself these men did it all the time and knew what they were doing and, of course, to trust in God. After four hours we were through the most difficult rapids. I discovered later it is here where the equator crosses the Negro River.

The little settlement, at the mouth of the Isana River was called Vila Isana. The original settlers were Spanish who chose to remain there after Colombia surrendered this territory to Brazil. Two brothers and their families lived here. Senhor Valentim, the older brother, was also Senhor Augusto's father-in-law, who had left me in his care in a shed on the waterfront. There I was alone again wondering what I would do next. I had an outboard motor and gasoline but didn't have a canoe.

The younger brother Senhor Fortunato, was the agent for the Panair Airline which landed at Vila Isana twice a month. He received small packages of mail sent to John and Dorothy Stahl who lived three days' travel up the Isana River. He told me he had sent a package of mail just a few days ago with some Indians and if I followed by outboard motor I might be able to catch up with them. I knew there was a letter in the package asking John and Dorothy to meet me at Vila Isana soon after receiving it. I should go as quickly as possible.

I approached Senhor Valentim. "Do you have a canoe I could rent to go up the Isana River for about two weeks?" I asked him. "Yes I do, but it needs some repair work done on it. I will have it done right away," he replied.

There was a long white sand beach in front of the settlement. The black water of the Negro River flows down from Colombia and Venezuela. When the murky headwaters of the Orinoco River in Venezuela overflow, the water runs into a canal which empties into the Negro River. This natural canal joins two of South America's largest rivers. Consequently the water in front of Vila Isana becomes much lighter.

The day finally arrived when, with rented canoe and my own outboard motor, I sailed into the Isana River.

CHAPTER SIX

IN THE TRIBE

When the Indians at the mouth of the Isana heard I was going to Seringa Ropita, and I needed to get there as fast as possible. They sent their chief Julio Americo, who spoke Portuguese, with me. He was well acquainted with the river and knew how to operate an outboard motor. It was late in the afternoon by the time we began our trip up the Isana River.

On the equator the sun rises at six and sets twelve hours later. All the local people set their clocks by the sunrise. Night falls very quickly after the sun drops behind the trees. Just before sunset I asked Julio Americo to take control of the motor, while I had some hard crackers to eat. After I was done I took the motor again and he had some himself; I noticed before he started to eat he bowed his head and returned thanks. Then I remembered I had not left any outward expression of gratitude to God before I ate. I felt ashamed of myself. There I was, the missionary, coming to teach them and I hadn't shown as much gratitude as this man had.

We traveled on until the sun had set and the full moon shone brightly. I told Julio that I would like to travel as far as possible after dark, if he was willing. Julio kept the motor going steadily until we arrived at the port of a village where he suggested we spend the night. "Sr. Henrique, wait here while I go up to the village to ask where we can sleep," he said as he started up the bank. Before long he returned saying, "Senhor Henrique, they want you to sleep here in the shelter on the bank and I'll sleep with them in the village." He took my hammock and tied it up in the small shelter and left for the village. I got in the hammock and had relaxed only a few minutes when Julio returned and said, "Senhor Henrique, they want us to sing with them."

"Who wants us to sing?" I asked wearily.

"The people in this village are having their evening meeting, and want us to join them." he replied.

We joined the group of about forty or fifty in their hut, seated on low benches. They were singing, in their own language, *What a Friend we have in Jesus*", "*There is Power in the Blood*" and many other well known hymns, all translated by Sophie Muller. Then they wanted me to preach to them. Since they knew very little Portuguese, Julio interpreted for me and we had a wonderful evening. They were very responsive and eager to learn more about Jesus. I was thoroughly blessed. That was my introduction to the tribal people on the Isana River.

The farther we traveled up the Isana River the worse the gnats became. We did not notice them when we traveled, but when we stopped, they swarmed around us and immediately attacked us. The women and children wore long-sleeved dresses to protect their arms. Some of the men swatted their backs with the broad side of their machetes.

Several mornings later as I churned my way around the last bend, I could see John and Dorothy Stahl on the river bank. They had heard the sound of an outboard motor and came to meet it.

John and Dorothy Stahl with their little daughter Caroline had lived at Seringa Ropita long enough to get to know the people and to build themselves a comfortable house. They gave me much information about the Indians and their culture during the few days I stayed with them. Their former co-workers had started to build a house for themselves nearby. When it became apparent they wouldn't be able to become part of the team among the Baniwa people, they had stopped the construction and left. There it stood. The thatch roof drooped sadly and its rugged, unfinished mud walls beckoned someone to finish it and move in.

"Henry, why don't you ask the Indians to finish the house for yourselves, while we go to Manaus. It will be ready for you when we return from the conference in Manaus." John suggested.

Before I left Manaus, our field director told me he had written a letter to the Stahls several months earlier asking them to attend the Mission's first conference in Manaus. He wanted me to encourage them to return with me. They were glad to accompany me and we made plans to have the Indians finish the house for us.

"That sounds like good advice, John." I remarked as I sized up the situation.

Immediately, I began working on the doors and windows. I called for five men to put new palm on the roof.

"How many days will it take the five of you to get the palm from the jungles and replace the old?" I asked the leader. After huddling together for several minutes, the leader of the group said, "Sr. Ariki, it will take us about ten days."

"What would you like for payment for the work?" was my next question. "We have talked about it and if you agree we each want a gun," he replied, thinking it was fair payment.

24

"That is fine, I will bring you each a gun when I return from the conference in Manaus." Contentment was written all over their faces.

"How many of you want to repair the floor and make it smooth.?" I asked the group of men. Two men stepped forward and said, "We will do it for you." After they talked to each other for a while one of them told me they each wanted a hammock and yard goods to make dresses for their wives. The remaining men offered to put white clay on all the walls. They each wanted a large pot, one 20 kilogram bag of salt, fishhooks and line. I promised to bring them the merchandise they asked for in payment for their work. I told them it would be about four weeks before I would be back from Manaus.

We would have to leave within a few days in order to be in Manaus in time for the conference. And I was anxious to see my family again after being separated while I accompanied our belongings on the river boat from Belem to Manaus. Then a few days after arriving in Manaus I was on my way up the Negro River towards the Isana River. I was lonesome.

I also asked an experienced man to make me a canoe to use with my four-horsepower Swedish outboard motor. He was the chief of Tunui Village which is less than an hour's paddling down river. He said he wanted a gun and two good hammocks, one for himself and one for his wife. I told him I would need the canoe as soon as we would be back. "Can you have it done in four weeks?" I asked him.

"Yes, Sr. Ariki, I will do my best."

The trip to Manaus created another problem. A Bible conference had been scheduled one day's travel upriver from Seringa Ropita during the very time we would be gone for the field conference. To solve this John asked Olegario, the elder responsible for the conference, to come down river to see him. John explained to him he would not be able to be at the conference because his chief had asked him to go to Manaus.

"Then we will have it without you," said Olegario without hesitation.

"No," he told Olegario. "You cannot have it without me." John was reluctant to have them go ahead without him.

On hearing this tears filled the eyes of the young Christian leader. He had spent many weeks to build extra shelters for the anticipated people. He and the young men had worked hard to get the village all cleaned up and ready. Others had been hunting for several weeks so there would be enough meat for the occasion. Many of the young boys had been fishing much of the time. The meat had all been smoked and was ready.

John urged him to postpone the meeting for six weeks. Olegario could not withhold his disappointment. "I promise to be there after our return from Manaus", said John. "Please tell your people to wait for me." Poor Olegario returned to his village very discouraged.

In Manaus my wife and daughters had been waiting for my arrival. The conference proved to be very encouraging and challenging. Rus Garber, the director strongly stressed the importance of learning to speak the language of the tribal people. With new enthusiasm I took my family with me back to the Isana River and we began our ministry with the Baniwa tribe.

CHAPTER SEVEN

SOPHIE MULLER

Prior to our arrival, Walnie Kliewer, a fellow missionary, had worked for several years with the Nyengatu people near the mouth of the Isana River. He wasn't there now because his family had called him to be with his sick father in the United States. Walnie was a very friendly person, loved the people and learned to speak their language very well in a short time. The Nyengatu people enjoyed singing with him as he accompanied them on his violin. He was there by the time Sophie Muller made her second trip to evangelize the Nyengatus on the lower Isana River.

Sophie Muller, a pioneer missionary.

Sophie Muller had been in Colombia evangelizing the Curipaco Indians for three years when she decided to reach out to other tribes. She had heard of the Baniwa-speaking people in Brazil on the other side of a mountain range on the headwaters of the Isana River. The Baniwa and Curipaco languages are very similar to each other. Two Curipaco believers accompanied her to Brazil to begin her ministry there.

A few years later we were assigned to work in this region and heard the Indians tell of the time when Sophie first arrived in their village called Mattinhaipan, meaning - "Place of No Firewood."

The Indians had all been in their houses when a Curipaco man arrived and told them there was a white woman at the riverbank wanting to talk to the chief. The chief had gone down to the river to greet the white woman and Sophie had told them in Curipaco, "God sent me here to teach you about Him. He wants me to tell how you can go to heaven when you die." She continued, "God wants me to teach you how to read and write so you can read His message to you."

The chief pondered what he had just heard. Then sadly yet hopefully replied, "We know the way to the bad place but we do not know how to get to the good place. Come on up to the house and teach us." The chief did not take long to convince his people they should all listen to this strange white woman.

Sophie was given a small empty hut to stay in and as soon as she was ready she went to where the Indians were still all together talking about this stranger who had just arrived. Within a very short time Sophie was ready with a large syllable chart and began teaching them the four vowels of their language. Later on after sunset she began teaching them the story of how God created the world and people. They were eager to learn and made good progress in learning to read and write. Evenings they listened attentively to the Bible stories.

There was a problem, however. Many years ago one of the prominent Baniwa witch doctors had a vision in which he was told, by their god, they should wait for a white woman to come to them. This white woman would tell them how to get to the "good place" – heaven. How were they to know if this was the right white woman?

The older men of the village spent much time discussing this problem when one of them said, "Let us put poison in her food and if she doesn't die then we will know she is the right woman." Poison was the honorable way these people took revenge. They would secretly put poison into the food of their enemy. Now they would do this to find out if this strange white woman was the one sent by Yampirikoli, their god.

The chief appointed Antonio to do this. So, Antonio told his wife to prepare a good meal for Sophie and when it was ready he would take it to her. She took great care to prepare a meal of yams and some smoked meat the white woman would be sure to like. Antonio took the calabash of the hot food to Sophie. On the way there he took a hollowed out palm nut and removed a good portion of poison and put it into the food.

Sophie received the food gladly and returned thanks to the Heavenly Father and ate. After finishing the food she put the empty calabash on the ground beside her hammock. Then she prepared herself for the night and fell asleep in the hammock only to wake up a few hours later feeling very sick. Sophie threw up into the empty calabash and laid down and slept again. It was daylight when she woke up and saw a dead rooster lying next to the calabash.

All the men gathered early in the morning discussing Sophie. Surely she was the one they were to wait for. They decided to listen to what she was teaching because their god had sent her to them. They would tell all their people to study with her.

Sophie taught the Baniwa people in village after village. After teaching them in the first village she asked them if there were other villages nearby. "Oh yes, there is a village down river just around the bend."

"I will go there tomorrow."

As soon as Sophie woke the next morning she noticed the village was very quiet. Nobody was around, not even a dog. All the windows and doors were closed.

"Did they all leave after listening to me for these days", she wondered.

Down at the river bank she saw them all. The women and children were sitting in the canoes with their dogs and chickens. The men were standing on the bank holding their canoes with the toes of one foot to keep them from floating away.

"Where are you going?" she asked them.

The chief replied, "We are going with you."

Then Sophie remembered she had told them she would be going down river to the next village. They too, were eager to go. When they arrived she began teaching right away and the ones from the first village helped her teach. After all, they knew more than those in this village.

When it was time for Sophie to return to Colombia she told the Indians she would be back in six months and bring them some books to read if they really studied and improved their reading skill.

Six months later Sophie was back there with several hundred booklets, wondering if she would give out even one. To her great surprise there were no books left long before she finished visiting all the villages where she had taught. The Indians had been so eager to learn to read they taught all those who had started to study with Sophie. The booklets were small, consisting of regular sized pages folded twice with a condensed Old Testament story on each of 16 pages. They loved to read these stories over and over again. Everybody wanted to learn to read.

At another time Sophie made an unexpected appearance in a large village. Nobody was outside to greet her so she went to the big house and walked in. Inside she saw the men sitting in a stupor on low benches along the walls. In the center of the room was a table with large clay pots on it. She went to the tables and asked them, "Who told you to make this yalaki drink and become drunk?"

In unison the group replied, "The devil told us to do it." She had spent time teaching them that God did not like people to get drunk. They had a desire to do what God wanted them to do but the old desire had overcome them. Then Sophie tipped the pots with the drink in it on the dirt floor. The Indians made no objections. In fact, they learned their lesson and never made the drink again.

While Sophie was with the Baniwas they told her about the Nyengatu people living farther down river. Later she went there to teach them to read and write in their own language. By this time she had been on the Isana River for several months, with a Brazilian visa. One day Senhor Valentim, the local police deputy, came to arrest her for being in the country illegally and for preaching to the natives. He and his small posse had paddled their canoe up to the village to arrest Sophie. Feeling quite inadequate to the task of arresting a foreign woman, the police deputy drank too much alcohol and arrived on the scene in a drunken stupor. The posse, who knew better than to let him approach Sophie in such a condition, told the Indians of his plans. Immediately, the Indians whisked Sophie into hiding. Many years later this same police deputy told me how ashamed he was of the way he mistreated Sophie Muller. I offered to take a letter of apology to her but his regrets were not that sincere.

On another occasion an official of the SPI wanted to have a friendly encounter with Sophie while she was traveling up stream with several Indians. Sophie and the Indians, however, were afraid he wanted to capture her, so whenever his motor-powered boat was about to catch up with them, they quickly hid Sophie in the jungles and submerged the canoe in the water near the bank. He never did meet with her.

CHAPTER EIGHT

NEW EXPERIENCES

The conference in Manaus was over and the Stahls and our family boarded the amphibious airplane heading back to the mouth of the Isana River. From there we went by canoe and outboard motor. Our youngest daughter Arlene had her first birthday while we traveled for the first time as a family up the black waters of the Isana River.

We enjoyed the scenery. The never ending palm trees marched along the river bank and disappeared in the distance. Occasionally we heard the loud call of a thunderbird, trying to drown out the noise of the motor. Antonio, our Indian guide, told us the thunderbird sang because there was thunder in the distance. Sure enough, it didn't take long before a thunder shower was upon us; but we stayed dry underneath the palm roof over our boat.

Audrey and Joanne enjoyed every minute of the trip but were uneasy whenever we stopped at the Indian villages. We were glad John and Dorothy Stahl were with us to give us some helpful instructions.

"The Indians like to greet each visitor with a handshake," John told us. "Men always go ahead of the women, according to their culture. When they invite you into their huts, you sit down where they show you." John added, "Another important thing is you accept the manioc drink they offer. You don't need to drink much. It is better not to go snooping around in the house. If they like you, they will give you some fruit when you leave." True to their culture, they gave Betty a hand of ripe bananas and me a smoked fish. We were glad they were accepting us as friends.

The river was quite high during the month of September and all the rocks were well submerged so there was no danger. We sailed high over some of the worst low-water rapids. However, at Tunui, which was the last village before we reached Seringa Ropita, we had to portage over a high hill and down to the river again. While the Indian men, women and children carried our baggage, my family watched. The empty canoe had to be pulled by sheer force over the sharp, granite rocks. The Indians just loved this kind of activity and showed it by their whooping and hollering. After crossing the rapids at Tunui we traveled another hour to get to our new home at Seringa Ropita.

Rubber Tree Stump Village also known as Seringa Ropita.

The name Seringa Ropita is derived from a rock in the river which looks like a rubber tree stump. Beside it is another rock in the shape of an axe head. According to legend, a huge rubber tree had grown there. It had been cut down by some powerful legendary person, leaving behind the stump and the axe head.

Our new house looked much better with the new palm thatch, doors and shutters. The walls, inside and out, had been covered with white clay from the banks of a nearby creek. It looked quite liveable. For a while we all slept in hammocks. The girls just loved it. John and Dorothy had us over for meals so we could have more time for settling in. Within a few days our house began to look like home to us. A table and bench had been made from boards the Indians had sawed. A work table was built in the kitchen and a new kerosene stove stood there ready to be used. John and I had nailed the window screen in place to keep out bugs during the day and bats at night.

One morning John dashed over to our house saying Dorothy was very sick. She was pregnant and had developed some serious problems. They had decided they would seek medical help down river because they were afraid she would lose the baby.

As they frantically prepared to leave, Dorothy's condition worsened so they decided they would return to the USA for medical help. Since they would be gone a long time, they decided to get rid of their household goods, and start all over again upon their return. They left us their food and some household items. The items we couldn't use, they took down river to sell.

We had not been there two weeks when the Stahls left us to fend for ourselves in a new place, a new culture and a strange language. We had to dig in and get to know the people and their ways. Learning their language became of prime importance.

Henry, family and Anne Golias.

The new canoe was finished and delivered the day I went upriver to attend the Indians' Bible conference which had been postponed. We named the canoe *KOEKATO*, which means "message" in Baniwa. Betty and the girls decided against going up to the conference. They preferred to stay in our new home. Antonio, my language informant, went with me to guide me up the rocky Cuiari River. Since the canoe had not been ready earlier, I was late in arriving at the conference. It was dark when we docked in the rocky port, but Antonio guided the canoe without hitting a single rock.

While we were still a distance away from the conference, I saw a row of tiny lights snaking their way from the houses down to the riverbank. The Baniwas were there to greet me, many of them carrying small kerosene lights. When the motor was turned off I heard them singing a welcome song for us. Antonio told me they wanted me to greet each one of them, after which they would unload my boat. What a blessing it was to see these people gather like this to hear God's Word!

It was in this village where Sophie Muller had taught the Indians a very impressive lesson several years earlier when she tipped over the clay pot containing strong drink and poured it on the dirt floor. They never forgot the lesson.

Olegario took me to their large dining room and told me to sit down on a bench next to a high table. Presently a dish of food was set before me. The small kerosene light wasn't quite bright enough for me to see what kind of food it was. "I have come here to be a missionary," I told myself, "and I want to be a good one. I will eat what they set before me". After giving thanks, I started eating gingerly. There was a piece of meat I didn't recognize. The soup and the manioc bread were good but the meat was very tough. I chewed and chewed. Finally I swallowed it and almost choked on it. "No harm done," I hoped.

During the meeting that evening they introduced all the folks from the various upriver villages. After a short Bible meditation we all retired. They put me up in their small chapel, by myself. They didn't seem to want to sleep with a *yalanawi*, (white person), in the same room.

Next morning, before daylight, I heard singing in the different huts. This was to wake up all the people. Then they filed into the conference building for a prayer meeting. Many of them knelt next to the low log seats which had been hewn out by axe and were quite uneven and rough. The leaders prayed one at a time. Then others prayed too, but soon they began to pray simultaneously in low voices. It sounded like a chorus of praise and petition. All of a sudden their prayer meeting was over.

Baniwas preparing to serve a meal.

The meals were a ceremony. The women did the cooking and took it to the high tables in the center of the yard. The tables were high enough to be out of the dogs' reach. Beside them stood guards to fend off the dogs while the rest of us stood in a circle with our own empty plates. When all the food was finally ready, Olegario led us in a few choruses and thanked God for all the food, naming each separately. Breakfast was no exception. The village leaders took the blackened pots of gruel made of manioc flour and began dishing it out. Most of the gruel was quite tasty.

During the morning sessions of the conference we listened to the testimonies of the believers from the various villages. First, all the women came to the front of the room, many holding their babies, while they introduced themselves. Several had forgotten their national names, so they had to ask their husbands. One after the other they gave their testimonies, while nervously combing their long hair or twitching the buttons on their dresses. They spoke of their devotion to the Lord Jesus because He had taken away their sin and their fear. Testimonies were an excellent thermometer of the spiritual well-being of the Church.

The men came next. A variety of confessions were expressed and sometimes forgiveness was asked of another Christian brother. They talked about God answering their prayers in miraculous ways. One man was exuberant because his snake-bitten dog had been healed when he prayed for it. Several mentioned they had asked God to help them find game for the conference and He had answered A good number praised God for answering their prayers when they were sick. Finally, the church leaders took their turns in expressing their love and thankfulness to God for the way He had led them through the previous months.

The noon meal was served in the huge conference building which seated well over three hundred people. Olegario started by reciting Bible verses. They remembered a wealth of Scripture. They sang a few choruses before he said grace. A few of the men handed out the cooked meat with their bare hands.

The piece of meat I was given looked very much like the meat I had the night before. I was going to find out what had been so hard to chew and very difficult to swallow. I turned to Antonio, sitting next to me, "What kind of meat is this?"

"Oh, Senhor Henrique, it is turtle. It's very good. Do you like it?"

"Yes, I like it but I want to know what part of the turtle this is."

He looked at it and told me, "That is the turtle's tail." I examined it myself and noticed it was not only the claw-like tail but also the part underneath it, with a short piece of intestine attached! So that is what I chewed on in the dark! Too late now! Antonio graciously offered to exchange it for a different piece. It really did taste good and I had no problem swallowing it.

I taught them in the afternoon, with Antonio as my interpreter. How attentively they listened to new truths of the Word! It was such a blessing to see them hang on every word. They couldn't get enough! Later in the afternoon there was time for recreation. They had prepared for different kinds of sports like walking on round logs lying on other logs (to make them want to roll), arrow-shooting contests, and of course, soccer, which is Brazil's national game. Soccer had arrived in the jungles before the Gospel.

Henry R. Loewen

CHAPTER NINE

INVITATION FROM CURIPACOS

We were on our way home from the conference village on the Cuiari River and had just entered the slower waters of the Isana River when we saw a man waving at us from his small dugout canoe. He greeted both of us with a white man's handshake which he must have learned from traveling traders. Turning to Antonio he spoke with much enthusiasm. Soon Antonio turned to me and said, in Portuguese, "Senhor Henrique, Jose wants you to go and teach them in his village and have a Bible conference with them." Jose was a Curipaco believer from the headwaters of the Isana.

Jose is from Butterfly Village.

"Where is his village and what is its name?" I asked, "Is it far from here?"

Pointing at the outboard motor he asserted, "With this motor we could get there in four days."

"His village is called Makalowana," he added. Later on he told me Makalowana means Butterfly Village.

"He wants you to go to his village very badly," continued Antonio, "Because they have problems. They want to know what to do with his brother who has turned back to witchcraft."

"Piri," I said, Antonio was also called Piri, which means brother. "What do you think I should do, should I go?"

We had not lived on this river a month and I had been away at one Bible conference and now this man begged me to go far upriver to teach. I was overwhelmed. Could I leave my family again so soon? I asked God for wisdom.

"Antonio, please tell Jose I'll try to be there in two weeks. When Jose heard this, his face beamed with satisfaction.

"Jose, can you come and spend the night with me?" I asked him.

"I would like to but I must get back to my village as soon as I can to tell them you are coming. We will have to hunt and fish a lot to feed all the people that will be there," he replied. Then he started to paddle his one-man canoe upriver while Piri and I continued on home.

Everything had gone quite well with Betty and the girls while I was away. Joaquim and Dominga, his wife, whom our girls called Baba, grandfather, and Abu, grandmother, had taken good care of them.

During John Stahl's time in the Isana River he had the believers help him build a church building at Seringa Ropita which was filled every Sunday with believers from neighboring villages. They came, bringing their children, their food, their dogs and chickens for the day. Many from farther away brought hammocks so they could stay overnight and go home the next day.

That gave us a fairly large group to teach at night. Joaquim, my interpreter, loved to stand up front and teach them. He was a short fellow, always smiling as he stood there, barefoot. His balding head and a five o'clock shadow betrayed his mixed ancestry. One Sunday he spoke on a portion in Acts where it says, "Sit at my right hand, until I make your enemies a footstool for your feet." Ever since the Baniwas became believers they had been persecuted and ridiculed especially by those from other religions. Joaquim said Jesus, their Savior, was now sitting at Father God's right hand until He would make his enemies to be Jesus' footstool. He explained they were being persecuted for trusting in Jesus, but someday when Jesus would return their persecutors would become Jesus' footstool. Maybe it was an unusual interpretation but they found comfort in the fact that Father God cared for His people. The Baniwas knew it took courage to take a stand for Jesus and to face persecution. They encouraged one another to be faithful to God whenever unbelievers would ridicule them.

Later that same year Rus Garber, our mission director, came to visit us. We went down to Vila Isana to meet him when the amphibious plane arrived. With him came Mrs. Jean Dye, missionary in Bolivia, and Stan and Muriel Johnson who had been missionaries in China. We had a very good time of fellowship the three days it took us to arrive at Tunui. By coincidence Sr. Athayde, the agent for the Service for the Protection of the Indian, arrived at Tunui at the same time we did. Both Mr. Garber and Sr. Athayde wanted to get in touch with Sophie Muller who was in Colombia.

Upon our arrival at Tunui, the Indians quickly picked up our luggage and carried it up the steep hill leaving the official to carry his own. By the time he arrived at the top of the steep hill, he was quite out of breath and in a very bad humor. That night Sr. Athayde heard Mr. Garber preach through an interpreter using Sophie Muller's translation of verses teaching us to be subject to authorities.

In the morning the Indians picked up the official's luggage first and carried it down to the river. Turning to me he asked, "What happened to the Indians who ignored me yesterday and today they are all attention?"

"Sr. Athayde, last night in the meeting our director read from Sophie's translation of the Bible which teaches us to be submissive to government authorities." After a few moments of reflection he said, "In that case, if that is what Dona Sofia teaches, there is no further need for me to go upriver to track her down." He went down river that same day.

The Baniwa's greatest threat had been a religious leader who came from time to time to undermine their faith. He told them his followers were the only believers in all the world, and they should give up their new faith. He also told them the missionaries would soon be taken away, but, he didn't say who would take them away.

John Stahl had told me there was a need of teaching on the Lord Jesus' return for his church, because some had the idea if Jesus would be returning soon, there would be no need to plant crops any more. As a result, many of them were making very small gardens and were short of manioc for flour and bread. The traders, who traveled up and down the river, were unable to buy any more manioc products from them. I began to teach them about the Lord Jesus' coming, the necessity of taking care of their families and being busy for God while they waited for His return. The result was remarkable. The following year they had plenty to eat and a surplus for trading.

Not long after Senhor Athayde, the SPI agent for the Isana, wrote a letter to his superior in Manaus which he gave me to read. The following is an excerpt:

> "The cooperation Sr. Henry Loewen, and the other missionaries, working under his direction, are giving the Service, is of great value; among them the following stand out, which I mention without fear of being challenged: 1) The obedience and respect

the indigenous people have toward the authorities of this country represented by the Indian Protective Service. 2) The incentive to excel in agriculture, making the Isana River the largest producer of manioc for this municipality. 3) And most importantly, the majority of the Indians on the Isana River are now literate, without the missionaries having built boarding schools but by teaching them from village to village."

About the same time the mayor of the municipality wrote:

"Whom it may concern: I declare that the alphabetizing and evangelizing of the New Tribes Mission, a North American religious organization, is doing on the Isana River is of great importance in view of the results obtained in the development of the people of the area. Evangelism has served remarkably well in correcting many bad habits and customs, thus the Indians have gone through a real transformation. Vices are no longer practiced. They no longer smoke, drink or dance. They do not take things from anyone without permission. They no longer lie nor cheat the merchants like they used to do."

The day to leave for Butterfly Village finally came. Joaquim, my guide, told me we would run into many dangerous rapids. We would have to pull the canoe over enormous rocks. I decided to travel light to make the most possible speed, that is, if a four horse power outboard motor has any speed at all. It was, however, much faster and easier than paddling.

Shortly after sunset of our first day we stopped for night on the bank of the river. Joaquim gathered some dry twigs and leaves to start a fire. That was my first night out in the jungles and I had mixed feelings about it. Since there wasn't much room on this point of high ground, Joaquim tied one end of each of our hammocks to the same tree near the fire.

We had smoked fish and manioc bread before we crawled into our hammocks. Joaquim was sound asleep before too long while I was wide awake staring into the starlit sky with my mind in overdrive. "What am I doing here?" I asked myself. "A mere country boy from Canada in this howling wilderness, with only an Indian between me and certain destruction!" After awhile, I collected myself and took stock of reality. "I am on my way to a distant Indian village to teach God's Word to the new Curipaco believers."

Presently my thoughts were interrupted by a sudden noise. This sent my brain reeling again. What could it be? Was it a wild animal creeping through the underbrush? I felt goose bumps rising all over my body. Then came a frightening crash which struck terror into my soul. I jerked in my hammock and Joaquim stirred.

"Ariki," he said turning to me. "That was only a large dry leaf dropping from the top of a tall tree. Leaves get heavy with dew at night." What a relief!

Early in the morning Joaquim said he wanted to stop for a short while at the village a few bends upstream. We found the people very friendly. They invited us to their large communal house where we were offered breakfast. There was no table. On the floor sat a small earthenware bowl with some greenish gruel in it. Beside it was a flat basket with some pieces of hard manioc bread in it. The bread was in the shape of a pancake. I watched to see what Joaquim would do. He took off his old, sweat-stained felt hat, bowed his head and thanked God for the food. I did likewise, though I couldn't understand a word he said. Maybe he was praying I would be able to eat what they offered.

He broke off a small piece of bread and dipped it lightly into the bowl and took a small bite. Then he took a sip of *patsiaka*, a drink made of water and coarse manioc flour.

I followed Joaquim's example and broke off a small piece of bread. All around me the Indians watched this newcomer closely. Wasn't I dipping my piece of bread into the dish correctly? Then I bit off a small piece and I knew right away why they watched me so closely. Before I knew it, I coughed and choked as the red-hot pepper burned its way down my throat. They stood by with water for me to cool my mouth, but I was sure they secretly enjoyed my misery.

After a while I recovered and spent some time talking to those men who spoke some Portuguese. Some of them wore only a loincloth, others wore trousers but no shirts. In the background, I could see the women wearing skirts only. The children, of course, were naked.

I noticed most of the people had black spots on their skin. Some had them only on the faces, while others had them all over their bodies. Between the dark spots, the skin was an unhealthy faded brown. Later on Joaquim told me the skin condition was a disease which spread from person to person. He said it could be transmitted only from the blood of an infected person. If an infected person wanted revenge he could, at an opportune time, prick his own finger, put a drop or two of his blood into a *patsiaka* drink and serve it to him. They believed it also could be transmitted by blood-sucking gnats.

After a short time of prayer with the people we continued on our way.

41

The next place was an abandoned village. There were many well kept houses but no people. Joaquim said they had gone to work in Colombia to earn some much needed pots and yard goods.

There were many people on the large flat rocks at Spider Rapids waiting to greet us. The men came down to the river to help us pull the canoe through the roaring rapids while the women and children watched from a comfortable distance. These people seemed to have fewer clothes than those in the previous village, and what they had was tattered and very soiled. I went to see their new chapel where they worshiped God. They had painted figures of deer, tapir and paca on the walls. There were enough roughly hewn log seats to accommodate about thirty people. Time did not permit for me to teach them from God's word, but we prayed with them.

Two of the leaders of Spider Rapids Village offered to help us navigate the rapids farther upriver. They helped us through Star Rapids, Fish Rapids, Deer Rapids, Snake Rapids, and other lesser rapids, till we reached Devil's Rapids, the biggest of them all. There we unloaded everything and dragged the canoe along a steep path which skirted the raging rapids.

Rapids on Isana River.

When we arrived at Star Rapids, we found a ready audience. The patriarch of this village had decided to change his name to John the Baptist after he heard the Bible stories. He was a good leader even though he couldn't read. It was evident John the Baptist loved the Lord Jesus. His wife was just as enthusiastic about her new-found faith. They invited us to teach in the evening. They sat on the edge of their seats listening as I preached. After I had finished, I gave them opportunity to ask questions about the Word of God.

Everyone already knew why we were going upstream. Jose, on his return from asking me to go teach in his village, had told all the people along the river I would be passing by to go to Butterfly Village. John the Baptist begged Joaquim and me to stop in his village on our way back to have a few days of Bible teaching and a baptism. We agreed to this and set an approximate date.

John the Baptist saw us off at the river bank just above Star Rapids. As I looked back I saw him kneeling on the sand with his hands towards heaven. What a dear saint! He was praying for us just like Paul prayed for the disciples in the book of Acts.

We walked along a jungle path from Snake Rapids to Sunshine Village. Laurenco, the one-eyed chief, lived there. They offered to portage my canoe around the rapids and then insisted we stay overnight to teach them after their evening meal. These people were Curipacos, whose language is very similar to Baniwa. Sophie Muller had learned to speak the Curipaco language in Colombia. Later on, she evangelized the Baniwas using the same language. They all understood each other, although some words were quite different.

Joaquim interpreted for me and the people listened attentively. The little chapel was almost full. The men and boys sat on one side while the women with their babies and girls sat on the other. The seats were axe-hewn logs lying on top of short logs. In spite of the uncomfortable seats, they enjoyed the lengthy meeting. Several times I was ready to stop but they asked more questions which I answered, in spite of being very tired from the day in the rapids.

After the meeting Laurenco offered to guide me to the next village. Really, I didn't need a guide because there were no more rapids, but I thought he wanted a ride in a canoe with an outboard motor. He told me his sons and their families would follow paddling their own canoes. Laurenco thought somewhat highly of himself. After all, he was one of the most respected Curipaco chiefs on the upper Isana River. He had a number of sons and daughters. He told me when he was very young he lost an eye when a blowgun dart punctured his eye. He and his young friends had been trying to shoot their darts straight up in the air as high as possible. One arrow went so high he lost sight of it when it returned it hit his eye. Even though he had only one eye, he had become a good hunter, as well as a renowned witch doctor. Laurenco had a struggle when he first heard about God. He felt attracted to Jesus but he was so bound to the deceptive and powerful practices of witchcraft he continued to resist God.

One day I asked him how he came to believe in Jesus. With enthusiasm and joy twinkling in his one eye, he began his story.

43

.

CHAPTER TEN

LAURENCO'S TESTIMONY

When Sophie first came to my village to teach us, I, Laurenco, was the one to welcome her. All the men and women and many children of the village learned to read and write while I continued with my witchcraft. I thought I was too old to learn. I did not oppose them in any way. My brother believed in Jesus, and before long some of my sons accepted this new belief, but I resisted the longing in my heart. Sophie talked to me about my spiritual condition, and I became convinced witchcraft was from God's enemy the 'evil one', whom we call *inhaimi*.

Sophie would come once every six months. This gave me time to think about Jesus, about God and the Holy Spirit. I felt attracted to the truth of the Gospel, but I decided to leave it for the others.

One day when I heard that Sophie was coming again, I became deeply convicted that I was wrong in being a witch doctor, so I hastily buried all my witchcraft paraphernalia in a hole in a dark corner of my house. I did not go out to greet Sophie like I usually did, but remained seated in my house, feeling very miserable, while covering up my sins. When she greeted all the other folks she inquired about me. When she came to my house, I invited her in. She soon asked me when I was going to put my trust in Jesus like so many others had done. I said I would do it some time soon. When she questioned me about my witchcraft, I said I knew I had received it from the 'evil one'.

"When do you want to exchange your witchcraft for Jesus?" she asked.

After thinking a while I answered decidedly, "Today." I had been tortured enough by the enemy, and my heart yearned for the same peace all the others had. I went to the corner of my house and dug up my old leather pouch with its evil contents. Hesitatingly I clutched the small bag. "Yes," I told myself, "I'm going to get rid of this bag of the devil's goods."

It took me a while to get down to the river that flowed lazily around a wide bend in front of my village. I had been the highest authority in my village, until the Gospel came. Now there was a greater authority which I could not resist. I stopped on the white sand beach still clutching the small leather bag. I bent down to roll up my pants to the knees, and slowly walked into the water. I wondered what my old friends would think? How will I earn an extra machete or an axe if I stop blowing on my people when they are sick? These questions burned in my mind as I went deeper and deeper into the water.

Then the Holy Spirit told me if I would only believe in Jesus, all these questions would be solved. I had come to the point of decision. As I walked deeper into the river the water began lapping on my trousers so I stopped again to roll them up higher.

The devil was right there. He tempted me to turn back and continue my witchcraft. "No," I told myself, "I really do want to live up in glory with Father God after my life on earth is over."

By now the water was quite deep. Suddenly I received an inner strength. I hurled the small bag of evil into the middle of the river where no one would ever be able to find it. Never again would I deceive my people with them.

Then I was free! I walked out of the river with a light step and a weightless heart. I had obeyed and I believed in Jesus to save me from the evil one and to give me eternal life.

Then I received a deep desire to learn more about the One who was able to give me strength. I had surrendered my long-time evil practice and He filled me with a lasting peace instead. I began to attend all the meetings with the Christians of my village.

By then, many of them could read from the little books which told them in our own language about the true God who lives up in heaven. I learned to sing the songs which many of them already knew. I became a real part of the new church. But I thought I was too old to learn to read. After all, I had only one eye to see with while all the others had two. So I depended on my younger brother John to teach me the wonderful things of God. I grew in God and cooperated in the believers' efforts to spread the Word of God to others of my tribe.

CHAPTER ELEVEN

BUTTERFLY VILLAGE

We left Sunshine Village in the morning and arrived at Butterfly Village in the afternoon. The believers here were enthusiastic about their faith and loved God very much. The women sang while they spent hours grating manioc roots. Many came to the conference from neighboring villages to listen to the teaching of God's Word. Every house was crowded with hammocks; the river port was lined with empty canoes. They all brought their dogs, which sometimes got into vicious fights.

Lino, the father of many of the men at Butterfly Village, had two wives. His sons from both wives looked very much alike, but the sons of the one wife were more aggressive. Aprigio was one of the aggressive sons. He had gone to work for a wealthy trader and learned the Portuguese language very well. He also learned more of the national culture. When we arrived Aprigio took a liking to me and became a faithful friend. He helped me to understand his people and was always ready with good advice. Aprigio told me when his father was a young man, he and the rest of the tribe had eaten human flesh. Now Aprigio felt very sad his father and grandfather had never heard about Jesus. Aprigio was also the chosen leader of the church at Butterfly Village. His brother Jose was the one who had paddled downstream to beg me to come and teach them.

Aprigio was very helpful in many ways.

Their brother Paulo had also believed in Jesus and had walked with Him for some time when his oldest son got sick and died. He was so distressed he wanted to get even with whoever was responsible for his son's death. Since there were no more witch doctors in the region, he went to Colombia to consult a well-known shaman. After going into a trance, he told Paulo in order to appease the spirits he would have to exhume the body of the child at night when there was no moon.

Paulo became convicted about following the witch doctor's instructions. Even so, one moonless night, after a number of days of anguish in his soul, he gave in and went to his son's grave and began to dig in the sandy soil. Paulo was afraid of evil spirits and wondered what would happen if he stopped digging. He continued digging furiously, wiping the sweat from his forehead with his bare arm. He was getting closer to the dugout canoe which served as a coffin when he stopped to think about the whole matter, but his fear of evil spirits overpowered him. He kept on digging.

Then Paulo remembered when he had trusted in Jesus all his fears had been taken away. He asked himself, Why should I dig up my son's body when Jesus has delivered me from evil spirits and fear? Paulo leaned on his shovel and pondered for a while before he gave in to the Holy Spirit. Then hitting his breast he prayed, "Father God in heaven forgive me for following the evil way of the witch doctor."

After throwing the dirt back into the hole he had just dug, he resolved to return to his village and tell the church about his struggles. Paulo made up his mind to ask them to forgive him and to pray for him. The young church didn't know how to react to such a situation, so they sent Jose to invite me to come and teach them what the Bible said about these things. I told the believers when they trusted in Christ, He gave them the Holy Spirit to live in their hearts. He was there to teach them right from wrong and to convict them of sin, just like he convicted Paulo when he was digging up his son's body. The Holy Spirit living within us is stronger than the evil spirit which lives in the world. Christ came to this world to destroy the power and the works of the devil. Because of what Jesus Christ did for us on the cross we have victory over sin. I told them we must forgive one another and help one another to become strong in the faith. The result was they were reconciled one with the other. Paulo was comforted and again walked with God faithfully. It was a blessing to fellowship with those people.

The women had prepared much food for the crowd of several hundred people. All the wild pig, paca, monkey and fish had been smoked and preserved for a week or more. The wild meat was boiled, cut into smaller pieces and pounded into shreds in a mortar. Fish was not pounded. They simply broke it into small pieces. At mealtime the pounded meat was distributed by several men with their bare hands, into an assortment of plates. Two men gave each person a small gourd of dark, smoky meat. All could have manioc bread, some fresh and some dried, to go with the meat. Not having spoons for the soup they soaked it up with the dry manioc bread. Some had spoons but no one had forks. Knives were not needed because they all used their teeth. Several bottles of dried, crushed pepper were passed around to flavor their food. Some used so much pepper they had to cool their mouths by whistling air through their lips. Dogs sneaked around everywhere picking up every bone. When two or more dogs rushed to get the same bone, there usually was a fierce fight. Did they serve dessert? It may not have been sweet but it was equally satisfying after a meal. It mainly consisted of plain, coarse manioc meal mixed with water. Sometimes, they added the juice of the purple assai palm fruit, giving it a nutty flavor.

CHAPTER TWELVE

BAPTISM

Twenty-eight believers wanted to be baptized in Butterfly Village. I took time every day during the conference to teach them the meaning of baptism.

Laurenco was standing on the riverbank during the short baptism service expectantly waiting for his turn. He wanted to be the first one to follow God in baptism. After all, he was the chief of one of the largest Curipaco villages and he thought he should be first. He joined wholeheartedly in the singing and when Joaquim prayed he closed his eyes, just like all the others. It was quiet, by Indian standards, not even a dog yapped. The dogs had all been taken away into the jungles and tied up.

Silently wading into the waist deep water Laurenco stood ready to obey Jesus' command to be baptized. "On the confession and testimony of your faith we baptize you, Laurenco, in the name of the Father, of the Son and of the Holy Spirit," Joaquim's voice rang loud and clear in Baniwa, just before we immersed Laurenco in the black water of the upper Isana River the believers on the bank sang a song about baptism while waiting to see their family members baptized. When all twenty-eight new believers had been immersed, the church leaders welcomed them into their fellowship of believers.

Soon it was time for us to leave Butterfly Village. The whole village as well as those from other villages were gathered on the sloping bank of the river singing in their language, *"Till We Meet Again"*. I was deeply moved to see their appreciation of our ministry as they bade me good-bye, shaking my hand and patting me on my shoulder. They were rejoicing in the love of God and wanted us to come back soon.

Laurenco, the one-eyed chief, had already taken his place on the bow of my canoe and we began our return trip. Much as I missed my family, I would have been quite happy to remain longer with those new believers. Joy filled my heart as we made our way down the river. The time at Butterfly Village had been very rewarding.

Laurenco and several of his men, helped us take the canoe and its cargo around Snake Rapids before they left to go to their village. Because

I appreciated his help very much I offered to give him something for it, and asked him what he'd like.

"Oh, yes, Ariki, I want some eye glasses." Then, looking closely into my eyes he continued, "Look, you have two good eyes and wear glasses. I have only one good eye so I need glasses, too."

"I will buy glasses for you when I go to Manaus and send them to you. Can you wait that long?"

"Yes, I can wait because I know you will get them for me," he said.

He was soon hidden from our view by tall trees as he walked up the path leading to his village, while Joaquim guided our canoe through the turbulent waters below the rapids. The swift current took us rapidly as we went through the many rapids on our way out of Curipaco territory into Baniwa-land. Soon we reached Star Rapids where John the Baptist was waiting at the port. He ordered some of his sons to grab my baggage and carry it to the village. Then he asked another son to get into our boat and guide Joaquim through the swift water of Star Rapids.

The people of Star Rapids Village stood in line to shake my hand and tell me I had arrived at their village. I knew I had arrived and didn't need to be told, but that was their way of greeting each other and I was happy to be greeted like one of them. My goal had always been to identify with them, and certainly, that was part of it.

Their small chapel had been reserved for me to stay in and the meetings were to be held in a much larger building able to accommodate the people from nearby villages. I barely got my hammock hung and a few things organized when their gong was sounded for supper. By the time we were all finished with the customary meal, the sun had set and the kerosene lamps were lit. They had simple tin, cone-shaped lamps which were barely bright enough to cast shadows.

The second sound of the gong announced it was time to gather for the evening meeting. The church leaders sat on benches in front of the rows of sitting people where they could watch the people coming in. There were also policemen, who made sure of order. They carried a thin, six-foot stick mainly to chase away dogs, but they also used them to wake those who fell asleep during the meeting. Instead of a mud wall, the building had a stick fence for better ventilation as well as to keep dogs out.

"Ariki," John the Baptist approached me. "We want you to teach us tonight." I hadn't been on this river three months and all the people already called me Ariki, which continued to be my name through the years.

I was prepared and Joaquim seemed to be anxious to interpret for me. I spoke in Portuguese and he translated it into Baniwa. That evening I taught them about the Good Shepherd and His sheep. Most of them had never seen a sheep so I explained what a sheep was and how a shepherd took care of them in Bible times. They sat on the edge of their log seats taking in every word.

In their culture they showed approval with a simple "hoo". When I spoke to them that evening, the leaders especially said, "hoo", in high pitched voices. Old John the Baptist was very vocal in his approval and strung out his "hoos" considerably more than the rest of them. He too was a village chief and had to be heard. It sounded odd to me but he was serious.

They wanted to be baptized the next day just like those at Butterfly Village. The new believers seemed to understand the meaning of baptism. However, what they didn't tell me was that a number of them had already been baptized! I wondered if I should lecture them for this. I decided to just leave it alone. I couldn't undo what had been done. Their reasoning was that they wanted to be baptized by someone who followed God faithfully.

Some months before we arrived on the Isana River, the churches in Colombia, under the teaching of Sophie Muller, had sent a Curipaco elder and a small group of believers to the upper Isana River to baptize the new believers. While there the elder fell into adultery, without being discovered. Later on when the truth came out, the new believers felt betrayed and believed his baptism was invalid and asked me to baptize them.

It was apparent more teaching was needed and I just had to learn to speak their language to do it. It was later that same year our field director, Mr. Rus Garber, Jean Dye, missionary linguist from Bolivia, and another couple came to visit us to see how we were doing.

At one point Jean Dye asked me, "What are your goals about learning the language?" I had begun language learning and had a deep desire to be able to communicate well with the people I was learning to know. I told her, "I plan to be able to teach them without an interpreter in six months."

CHAPTER THIRTEEN

LANGUAGE LEARNING

The challenge of learning the language spurred me on to master the Baniwa. There were no study books available, so I listened, took notes and learned. The Baniwas, however, used some portions of God's Word in their services, which were translated by Sophie Muller, in a blend of Curipaco and Baniwa. I listened to them read during the evening meetings and noticed that whenever they came to a Curipaco word they would read it aloud in their own language, thereby giving me the opportunity to learn two languages at once.

Once, when we met Sophie Muller on the Colombian border, I asked her to give me something in writing to help me along in learning the language. What she wrote was very helpful even though it was written on a piece of paper the size of a regular envelope.

I was convinced God had sent us to the Baniwas for a purpose, and Betty and I spent much time listening to the Indians and having them correct us when we spoke. I got very impatient and wanted to be able to speak at once, so I learned patience in various ways. Often, when I would sit down to study, an Indian would come and wanted my attention. Only later did I realize the very ones who interrupted me and tested my patience were the ones who taught me something new about the language.

One day we got unexpected visitors from Venezuela. Ken Finney, a mission leader, came with Jim Barker who was working with the Yanowamo tribe in Venezuela. They had with them a Venezuelan fellow who spoke English quite well. Their main purpose was to see if there was any way in which they could go into the unreached Uaica tribe, also known, in Brazil, as Yanomamy. Jim Barker had become quite fluent in the tribe's language in Venezuela and wanted to make contact with the ones living in Brazil. They asked me to take them downstream to the agent of the Service for the Protection of the Indians, to get the proper permission to enter the tribal area which was under his jurisdiction. However, as accommodating as Senhor Athayde, the SPI agent was, he was unable to give them the needed permit. Since the men all needed to go to Manaus, we decided to go there in our twenty-eight-foot dugout canoe. We made the seven-hundred-mile trip in five long days.

It was a little easier to leave my family this time since Anne Golias had joined the team. She had spent a few years in Colombia with Sophie Muller and had a good knowledge of Curipaco, which is very similar to Baniwa.

When the Mission leader in Manaus saw me, he prevailed upon me to take off a few more weeks and fly to Vianopolis to attend the Mission's annual conference. It was very hard for me to make the decision because it would keep me two weeks longer away from my family on the upper Isana River. I did go and had a very profitable time with the other missionaries there as well as with a group of Bible school students, some of whom later came to work with us. I was concerned I wouldn't meet my six-month goal of getting enough of the language to teach without an interpreter.

I was very lonely for my family but as always the Holy Spirit reminded me He could take care of them much better than I. That comforted me but I was still very lonesome. When I returned, I found them all well and very happy to have me back again. They seemed to be much more precious to me after the two-month absence.

Language had priority and I worked at it long hours with an informant. I took every opportunity to teach the Baniwas, whether with an interpreter or in Portuguese. At times, these opportunities were far away from our station. On one short teaching trip I took Antonio along. He knew Portuguese quite well and was willing to travel with me and help me. He had been one of the first believers when Sophie Muller first came to teach them. He had grown much in the faith since he also had been John Stahl's informant. Then I began to notice that when I taught in Portuguese, Antonio didn't always understand and interpret exactly what I said. That drove me to even more language learning so I would not need an interpreter .

Eight months after I expressed my language learning goal to Jean Dye, I made another teaching trip and spoke without an interpreter in the first village above Snake Rapids. The palm-thatched shelter was packed with people and it was hot and muggy as I stood there in front of more than one hundred eager, brown faces. I spoke from Acts chapter four where the Apostle Peter spoke to the leaders of the Jews telling them there was no "salvation in any other: for, there is none other name under heaven given among men, whereby we must be saved."

The Holy Spirit worked as I struggled along in the language and all of a sudden a man stood up and began to tell me he wanted to believe in Jesus. I listened to him talk for a while and suggested he tell Jesus he wanted to trust Him. He did that and sat down. I continued with the Bible lesson and before long another person got up and expressed his desire to put his faith in Jesus Christ. There were a number of others who also rose and expressed their desires to be saved by Jesus Christ.

With all these new believers there was much more urgency to teach. Joaquim, my faithful helper, was with me on that trip and he taught in some meetings. By that time I could understand almost everything Joaquim said and he helped me understand whenever the Curipacos, of this village, asked me questions.

With God's help I understood more and more of the language and culture of the people and they accepted me as one of their own. What impressed them most was that I sat down with them and ate their food. Eating with other people meant fellowship and trust. When eating with them I could hear them talk about things relating to their personal lives and I paid close attention to the way they talked with each other.

On the return trip we stopped at a village where there were a few very new believers struggling in the faith. They wanted to talk with Joaquim. It was a very hot afternoon and I was tired so they offered me a place to hang my hammock. Joaquim remained in the adjacent room and talked to them there. Through the thin walls I could hear them speak and at various times I heard the other man mention the name Zambo but I didn't know who this Zambo was. Later on when we were alone I asked Joaquim, "Who is this man called Zambo?"

He retorted quickly in an irritated tone, "Who told you about Zambo?"

"I overheard you when you talked to the other man when I was lying in my hammock," I admitted.

Knowing that Joaquim had a bad temper I did not pursue this any further but on another occasion it came out that Zambo was his tribal name and no white man was supposed to know it. They were very careful not to use their tribal names in the presence of outsiders. Therefore, whenever they told us their names they only gave us their Brazilian names. From time to time, however, some child would forget and use his sibling's tribal name in our presence. Some names were very flattering while others were not.

Over six hundred people attended the conference at Tunui, a short distance from our station. Every house was full and the numerous temporary shelters all around the village were crowded. Tunui was located on a high plateau at the end of a twenty-mile long mountain range. Huge boulders extend to the other side of the river causing rapids very difficult to navigate every season of the year.

Baniwas gathering for meal during conference.

Their large chapel was much too small for all the conference guests. A new and larger building had been erected to serve as a meeting place, and even that was crowded. The whole chapel was a sea of people. The young people gathered in groups in different areas to talk and laugh but when it was meeting time they all attended.

One night there was a brawl when one of the girls gave some "love potion" to the young men. This potion made from roots of certain plants has a stimulating effect. She wanted only one particular young man, to whom she had taken a fancy, to drink it. Unfortunately however, the love potion was, unknowingly, consumed by a number of young men arousing them all to commit fornication with her. After things died down, the church leaders dealt with the problem. The girl married the one she had desired.

More than a dozen villages were represented at the Tunui conference. Some had come from Colombia and a few from Venezuela. Each morning there was a session when all the believers from one particular village gave their testimonies. This dragged out the conference to over five days. In spite of the large crowd there was plenty of food, though, mostly smoked game and fish.

Seventy-two believers had come there to be baptized. At that point the church was still feeling the effects of the adulterous elder who had baptized many believers. They wanted me to do the baptizing. I was able to persuade them to allow several of the more mature elders to help me with the baptizing; otherwise, it would take far too long. Everyone was satisfied. Over time, I gradually turned the responsibilities of all baptisms over to the native elders.

CHAPTER FOURTEEN

INDIANS' HEALTH

It was a beautiful day on the Isana River. The sun was shining brightly and a gentle breeze was blowing through the window screen keeping the ever-present gnats from forcing their way in. It was between rainy and dry season. The river was still quite high, but was flowing at a much slower speed. The huge trees on the mountain side across the river were bright with yellow and pink blossoms. Such was the day as we sat around the table ready to eat lunch.

Then, one of the girls saw a canoe full of people pulling into our port. We all strained our necks to see if, maybe, we knew them. Yes, one of them was Laurenco's son. We wondered who the others were and what they wanted? As we kept on looking we saw two men carry a sick person in a hammock tied to a long pole. One strong man was at each end of the pole as they walked up the bank toward our house. Silently I prayed, Oh Lord, help me to give them whatever help this sick man needs.

A variety of parasites with different symptoms had been a constant health problem in this tribe. One of them caused folks to turn yellow and weak. Eventually many died from it. Of course, they did not know what the cause was nor how to treat it. We had obtained medicine from the State's health department to treat them. This had been so successful that, unfortunately, the Indians began calling me a witch doctor.

Through the years the Indians have believed any sickness to be caused by poison. This was cause for much suspicion among them, especially toward strangers. They had perfected some very formidable poisons, made secretly from roots and vines. Nobody knew who had poison and who didn't. As a result, everyone was suspect.

Whenever somebody would serve them the traditional *patsiaka* drink they were suspicious. When anyone stopped in another village, the owner of the house would ask his wife to prepare the *patsiaka* drink, and when it was ready she would give the gourd with the drink to her husband who then would stir the drink and take a sip or two to prove to the visitor the drink was safe and there was no need for suspicion. If the visitor then would give his host a few bananas, the host would accept them and just lay them aside and later inspect them very meticulously to check for any possible poison.

Whenever anyone would get sick, they thought he was poisoned and tried to find out who might have done it. Everyone was always a suspect.

They were also afraid witch doctors would place a curse on a person and he would get sick. When this happened they would consult another witch doctor who would tell them what to do and how to appease the evil spirits and so cancel the curse.

One of such diseases had the symptoms of hookworm infestation which left the person anaemic and yellow. They did not have a cure for it, and so feared it greatly. All we did was give them an antiparasitic treatment followed by blood-building pills. That would usually take care of the infestation and the symptoms in a short time. No witch doctor was able to do this so they would come to us. We lost count of the thousands of pills we gave out and of how many people had been helped.

I recognized the man who greeted us through the window as being the oldest son of Laurenco, the one-eyed chief, from Sunshine Village. He told us he had brought his brother to be treated. I told him they could hang his hammock in the newly built shelter for sick people.

Betty and I prayed for wisdom to treat this very sick person before I went to look at his condition. It looked like a typical, well advanced case of hookworms but I was hesitant to give him the toxic treatment before he gained some strength. After explaining to him how I was going to treat him he was confident he would get well. I felt he needed help quickly so I gave him injections of blood builder and vitamins for a whole week. Then I gave him several small doses of antiparasitic capsules. A few days later he told me he felt a little stronger, but I kept on giving him the blood builder. In two weeks he was strong enough to get up to walk around, and a week later he asked his brother to take him home.

One Sunday afternoon after Bible study a man from another village came to my wife and gave her several oranges. Later, when she began to peel one of them an Indian stopped her and told her to throw it away. In a whisper he told her they could have been poisoned. Betty disposed of them; we never did find out whether they were really poisoned. They were always suspicious, and we knew that God was watching over us.

With the coming of the Gospel many Indians believed in Jesus and were freed from these fears while others continued to live in constant distrust.

We were especially sad when one of the staunch old believers got sick and told his family he had been poisoned and would die. This fear of poison had been rooted into their lives so deeply that many had an extremely difficult struggle to overcome it. The enemy of the Gospel was doing his best to keep the hearts and minds of the new believers darkened by their former fears. We spent many hours teaching the people, individually and collectively, about disease, cleanliness and the ways diseases could be transmitted. Ever since they first had contact with civilization there have been many cases of tuberculosis among the Indians. They believed it was a slow-acting poison without a cure. Many died of it.

A young lad in Tunui lost his mother when he was young. His father remarried but he stayed with his grandmother. He was tall and thin and healthy when we first met him. He wasn't shy about sharing his belief in Jesus. He had learned to read and write along with all the others in his village. His grandmother couldn't read but she had believed in Jesus ever since she first heard about Him. Her grandson would read to her, help her in the garden and fish for her.

One day, he began to feel weak and sickly and started to cough. He spent more and more time in his hammock just reading the portions of God's Word. His grandmother took very good care of him as he got weaker and weaker.

One morning he called her in his weak voice, "Grandmother, they are calling me."

"Who is calling you," she asked.

"The 'good ones' are calling me," he answered.

Alarmed, she quickly went to him and asked, "Are you going to them?"

"Yes, grandmother, I'm going," he replied as he closed his eyes and passed over into the presence of the Savior whom he had loved.

Over and over again the Indians asked me to get them some medicine to take away the dark blotches on their skin. And, every time I'd go to Manaus I'd seek out the State Health authorities and ask them to check out the ugly disease.

When, finally, a team was sent up to our station to take skin samples of as many people with blotches as possible, I sent out word to the Indians to come to our station. They came by the hundreds with their families and dogs. The health technicians took tiny skin samples of hundreds of infected men, women and children.

Several months later they sent word that they knew what it was and how to treat it. Again I sent out word to the Indians for them to come and get their treatments. Many, when they saw it was an injection, wanted to turn back but others persuaded them to stay. By the time the technicians left, they had treated close to one thousand people. They left enough medicine for us to use on those who had been unable to come. It didn't take long before we noticed their skin blotches were becoming fainter and their skin returned to its natural color. Then those who hadn't previously come now showed up for their injections. They all wanted to be clean again.

Madalena from Tunui had so many blotches in her face it was almost black. She was a very kindhearted woman, always helping others. The treatment cleared up her face completely. She would always sit and listen while Antonio, her husband, helped me with translation work. During one short break I asked her to tell me how she first heard about Jesus. Her face lit up as she began.

Henry and Madalena. She was a precious woman.

"I lived in Tunui with my two boys after their father passed away. They grew up and helped me very much in my garden and fished and hunted for me. One day Lauriano, the oldest son, came to tell me he was going to go to Colombia with some other men to work to buy some much needed clothes, some pots and pans and other things for the family.

"Then, one day, several months later when I was cleaning a fish in the creek down behind our house my son arrived home. He told me he had looked all over the village for me but hadn't been able to find me. Then he asked me. 'Mother, what are you doing?'"

"I was puzzled. Why would he ask me what I was doing when he could see it. I wondered if he was drunk or if he had lost his mind. "'Son, I am cleaning a fish.'"

"During his time in Colombia he came in contact with a local Curipaco man who invited him to go with him to a certain village where a white woman was teaching about God. Several weekends they went to listen to the white woman who spoke, in their language, about a God who created everything and loved all people.

Henry and Lauriano. He was one of the first believers.

"Lauriano couldn't understand all of it but he had a deep desire to share this with his mother. So, he decided to return home. He asked me another question which made me more convinced something was wrong with him. "Mother," he asked. "Where did you get the fish?"

"Now I knew he had lost his mind for sure because he knew where fish were caught, but I answered him, "Your step-father caught it in the river." Then he told me he now knew who made the fish and the river, the forest and all the game. He told me all about the white woman who told him about God and His Son Jesus and that He wanted all people to believe in Him so they could go to be with Him in heaven after they died."

Tears filled Madalena's eyes. She didn't want to show that she was moved but could not restrain herself.

She continued. "My own son was the first one to ever tell me about God."

CHAPTER FIFTEEN

SUSANNE

Two years passed very quickly with all the activities and excitement. More excitement was in the air when we got word that Susanne Plett and her cousin Elizabeth Koop were coming to see us before they were to go on furlough to Canada.

They had been working in the Marubo tribe deep in the jungles. To get there they had to walk overland for several days through swamps and creeks, a potential for painful blisters on their feet. During their time in the tribe they lived together in one house. They worked hard at learning the language and the culture of the tribe. Their co-workers lived in their own house a short distance away. Soon they acquired a small dog to be their companion and to warn them of any visitors. When they were preparing to leave the tribe to go on furlough, they needed to dispose of their faithful little dog. They didn't want to leave it with the Indians, and their coworkers Bob and Ruth Allen, didn't want it. That left them with only one alternative - to put him to sleep. Some of the Indians, unfortunately, saw them perform this unpleasant task. Dogs have an important place in their culture. They would never kill them although they might starve them half to death. But, that was different.

A curse was, consequently, placed on the ladies as well as on Bob and Ruth for violating the Indian culture. They predicted Susanne would die soon and that her cousin would get married. Of course, the missionaries dismissed it because they trusted in God for protection.

We were all excited as we watched the amphibious plane land in the middle of the Negro River at Vila Isana near the mouth of the Isana River, and taxi towards a buoy near the bank. As soon as the waves died down, a few of the local men paddled a large canoe to the plane to pick up the passengers. Two ladies and a man stepped into the canoe.

It turned out that John McCulloch was coming to see us, too. That meant our boat would be heavily loaded since we were going to take our supplies with us also. After a brief visit with the local people, we began our trip back to our home upriver at Seringa Ropita.

With the extra weight in the canoe and going upstream our progress was slow. Instead of staying overnight only once, we spent three nights in different villages. Each night we taught the Word of God to a different group of believers. When traveling we always taught the people in their evening meetings.

News travels fast along the river and before long everybody knew we had visitors from another country. Early Sunday morning our place began to fill up with people. They came from upriver and down river. Unbelievers from distant villages came to see these white strangers. The church elders took the opportunity to teach them the way of salvation.

For the mid-day meal we gathered in a huge circle in the yard while the food was placed in the center. Then they prayed and served the food. They tried to keep their dogs at bay, but still, they sneaked fish bones and other morsels. When two of the dogs would aim for the same bone, a fight would break out. Women and children would get up and escape as fast as they could while the men screamed and yelled at the dogs, trying to stop them. Then the meal would continue, until the next dog fight.

The unbelieving Indians lived farther away so, late in the afternoon, they got their things together to leave. One lady, before she left, took a few leftover bananas to Susanne for a gift. The crowd was thinning out but there were several families from the nearest village who wanted to stay for another meeting before leaving. It had been a very busy day. After dark, when the last ones left, we were exhausted.

We had a very pleasant time with Susanne who was from Betty's home church. It was Susanne who had given us the final challenge to enter mission work. The days slipped by quickly.

Late one night Susanne came to our house. She had a severe stomachache and asked for some medicine to relieve the pain. She thought her pain was from the antiparasitic which both she and Elizabeth had taken a few days earlier. Early in the morning we went to our co-worker Anne's house and found that Susanne had not slept well at all. Before long all our pain medicine was gone and her pain became more severe. For several days we prayed she would recover. But she only got worse. At one point she asked me to pray with her, because she felt she wouldn't live. Our only hope was in God and we committed our ways to Him again. She herself, prayed God would do that which would glorify Him most.

In the meantime the Indians from the nearest villages come to see how she was doing. They had been talking about Susanne's illness and believed she had been poisoned.

"Somebody gave her some bananas. Maybe they were poisoned," they remembered.

"Yes," they said. "That must be it. Her symptoms seem just like poisoning. But, we can't tell that to the missionaries because they don't believe our people do that."

"No," they told each other. "She will die because there is no antidote for the poison."

Susanne's condition got worse every day. Her feet were badly swollen and she vomited vile stuff. We concluded she had a bowel obstruction. We realized there was nothing more we could do for her. It was up to God to heal her.

In a few days the bi-monthly plane in which she had arrived was due to land at the mouth of the Isana River. Should we consider taking her there to go for medical help? We talked it over and prayed for wisdom. We knew the trip would not be easy for her. However, Susanne said she would like us to take her down river in our boat to meet the plane. Betty and I didn't really think it was wise but we agreed to take her. We discussed it with Joaquim, our constant helper.

"What do you think, Joaquim? Shall we take Susanne to the mouth of the Isana River to go for medical help?"

"I don't know what to think, Ariki, she is very sick," he replied. Then he added, "If you think you should take her then I will help you." That settled it. We would take her, the sooner the better. Anne, our co-worker, supplied an air mattress and pillows. We quickly readied the canoe. Then Betty came down to the river and informed us Susanne was sleeping and it would be better to wait until she was awake.

Walnie Kliewer, who was stationed at the mouth of the Isana River among the Nyengatu people, was visiting our station for a few weeks. He and John McCulloch were staying in John Stahl's vacant house. Both of them would be going with us to take Susanne down river. We carried Susanne down the slippery slope to the canoe. Since the gnats were bad, we covered her face with netting while she waited for the rest of us to board. Joaquim prayed and then we were on our way.

Within about half an hour we arrived at the violent Tunui rapids. The villagers came to the river to meet us and we discussed with them the possibility of shooting the rapids. They suggested Susanne should stay in the boat but everything else be removed to lighten the load. Suddenly Susanne had an excruciating seizure of pain. This delayed our departure until it subsided.

Four men with large paddles took us through the raging waters, two on the bow and two on the stern, while another handled the outboard motor. I sat next to him.

The men on the bow guided the boat. Even before we hit the rapids we were already navigating the threatening swells of the river. I had to trust their judgment and skill while Susanne lay on the air mattress apparently oblivious to everything. We were gaining speed, aiming for the rushing water between two rocks rising above the water. In a matter of seconds we sailed through the channels and hit white water with its unpredictable waves and underwater rocks. Suddenly we were in calm waters. We had made it!

The water was eerily quiet as we continued on below the rapids. We wondered whether this was the calm before the storm. In the distance there was a small dugout canoe.

By now I operated the motor with Walnie beside me. Joaquim and John McCulloch were up front, with Elizabeth beside Susanne. Traveling around bend after bend I wondered if we would be able to pass the last rapids before dark. The sun was quite low when Elizabeth called me to come quickly.

"Henry," she said tearfully. "Susanne is going!" I quickly put my fingers to her wrist and found her pulse was fading away. And then she was gone!

Since it was my boat and motor, I was in charge, I motioned to Walnie to turn the canoe around and go back. It seemed so final. There was nothing else but to give in to the grim reaper. In a few minutes we reached a village where we stayed overnight. I offered to stay in the boat, with the body, while the others went up to the village to sleep. I didn't look forward to it, but somebody had to do it. During the night I wrote a letter to Susanne's parents. I had paper and envelopes in my briefcase. John McCulloch would mail the letter in Manaus. I also wrote a letter to the British Consul in charge of Canadian citizens and one to the director of our mission.

Susanne Plett

May 15, 1956

Dear Mr. and Mrs. Plett,

Precious in the sight of the Lord is the death of his saints. Psalm 116:15.

Your daughter Susanne and Elizabeth Koop came to visit us here on the Isana River a few weeks ago. We enjoyed Susanne's company very much. Two weeks into their visit Susanne took very ill. Even though we did all we could to treat her and relieve her of suffering, she only got worse.

We prayed much for wisdom from God to know if we should take her on the long, hard trip to catch the next plane to Manaus. After we all felt at peace about it we left the mission station. Susanne was propped up as comfortably as possible in our boat. We had to pass a set of bad rapids where she got quite a jolt. After a while she calmed down and we kept on traveling.

Elizabeth did not leave her side at all. About five thirty p.m. she called for me and said Susanne was going. I quickly asked another missionary to handle the motor and I went to sit down next to her, but she did not recognize me.

She breathed her last at six fifteen o'clock this afternoon, the 15th of May, 1956. She was unconscious about an hour before she passed away.

While she was alive, her lips never ceased to praise God who had redeemed her.

We are going to bury Susanne at the mission station in Seringa Ropita on the Isana River.

Your brother in Christ,

Henry Roland Loewen

P.S. Please let my parents read this letter.

We resumed our trip early in the morning and before long the people at Tunui saw our boat from a long distance. They knew Susanne had passed away. Just below the rapids the women and children took our luggage over the hill while the men tied long ropes to the boat and began pulling it through the relentless rapids. Going upstream through the rapids took a lot of time. We spent no time talking to the people but immediately continued on to our station. At home, too, we saw them watching us from a distance. They also knew Susanne had died or we wouldn't be back so soon. A number of people were following us in their canoes.

The chief from Tunui helped me make a coffin for Susanne. Interestingly enough, we used the same boards she watched being planed by hand a few days earlier. She had stood there a long time trying to communicate, in some way, the love of Jesus, to a man who knew very little Spanish. Late in afternoon we buried Susanne in a small clearing across the little creek where some children had been buried. It didn't take the men long to dig the grave in the sandy soil.

Joaquim and I each gave a short message at the grave side, the Indians sang a song in their language. All of us missionaries sang *"Beyond the Sunset"* at Susanne's request, while the last rays of sunset painted the few stray clouds in the sky.

Beyond the Sunset, O blissful morning,
When with our Savior heav'n is begun.
Earth's toiling ended, O glorious dawning;
Beyond the sunset, when day is done.

> Beyond the sunset no clouds will gather,
> No storms will threaten, no fears annoy;
> O day of gladness, O day unending,
> Beyond the sunset, eternal joy!

- Virgil P. Brock

CHAPTER SIXTEEN

SCHOOL

There was hardly a day when some Indian didn't ask for a school in their village, so great was their desire to learn more. I said I would write to the mission leadership to ask for teachers to be sent up here.

In due time Myrtle Rehn and Norma Aren came to teach the Indian children. They prepared new primers in the language and adapted Portuguese primers. They spent a month or so in each village. Most parents however, needed their children to help in their plantations. They couldn't let them study. The teachers informed the leaders of the villages the children must be able to study without interruptions. In dozens of villages they built schools. Unfortunately, there were not enough teachers for all of them and, eventually, some of these school buildings fell into disrepair. Soon the children read quite well in their own language and began to understand Portuguese.

It wasn't easy for the lady teachers. Living conditions and the food were not what they were used to. The children were no more used to schedules than they were to a pencil, but they all wanted to learn. Most of them applied themselves very well.

There were also some adults who wanted to learn to read and write. John the Baptist couldn't read, because he said he was too old. He was a good chief, a good leader in the church and had been chosen to be an elder even though he was unable to read. He knew a lot of the Bible and the Spirit of God taught him. He would ask one of his sons to read the Scripture so he could teach.

One older man teaching another to write.

When I spent a week with him I confronted him about learning to read. "No, Ariki," he said. "I'm too old to learn to read. Let the younger ones learn to read."

"Don't you want to be a stronger church leader and be able to teach better?" I asked him.

"Oh yes, I want to be strong for God and I want to be able to teach better."

"Then, it would help you very much if you knew how to read, don't you think so too?"

"Yes, Ariki, I would like to, but I'm too old." In the end he agreed to let me teach him.

We began right away. The primers the ladies had made were a big help. I began with showing him some syllables. Patiently I showed him the various combinations of syllables and how they made words.

"Now I see how words are made, this one is *nopana*, (my house). Let me try some more."

"I can read," he exclaimed with satisfaction.

I spent only five days with him and he was reading from the Baniwa New Testament.

Several months later I asked John the Baptist to accompany me on a long trip to the headwaters of the Isana. I always made it a point to take promising church leaders on my teaching trips so I could mentor them. On the way we stopped in at every house and shelter along the river. We would visit with the people a while and then I'd read a portion of Scripture with them. After a brief explanation of the portion I prayed with them. John the Baptist was all attention each time and voiced his approval with his peculiar hoo hoo's.

Three or four stops later after I finished reading and praying he said, "Now it is my turn to read." Why had I been so thoughtless and not invited him to read and pray with his own people? Maybe I had been too concerned with teaching the people something new and hadn't seen the opportunity.

"That's a good idea," I agreed. "Just go ahead."

He stood up in his bare feet, opened his New Testament at Matthew chapter 11 and began reading verse twenty eight. "Come unto me all ye that labor and are heavy laden, and I will give you rest." He read to the end of the chapter, closed his Book and led in prayer.

"Now we can go," he said with satisfaction.

After that I let him read and pray with the people in every village we stopped at.

Once a year the religious leader made a trip up the river to recruit children for his school, not far from the mouth of the Isana River. He had opened this school soon after Sophie Muller began teaching and evangelizing there. It was a boarding school run by in their traditional way. The parents who let their children go to that school didn't like the changes they saw in them when they returned home. They said the children were confused and didn't know whether they were Indian or *yalanawi*, white man.

They also came back with a bad attitude towards Christians. On occasions the religious leader would have with him a group of students from the school. While he talked with the people of the village, the students would rummage through the houses gathering all the evangelical books they could find. Hiding them under their shirts they would sneak them to the boat. Later on these books were burned.

The believers didn't want to send their children to the other religious mission school so they continued to beg us to open more qualified schools. Our aim, as a mission, was to teach them to teach others. We began by teaching government approved courses to the most intelligent ones hoping they, in turn, would teach their own people.

Adauta Nascimento, a young lady missionary who was also a qualified Brazilian school teacher joined our team. She registered one school with the municipal board of education and improved the level of education. Her pupils came from different villages and many stayed all week living with local families. After a few years some finished the prescribed course and were hired by the municipality to teach in their own villages under Adauta's direction. Before long dozens of official schools were opened along the river, taught by their own people.

Later several went to Manaus to finish high school in an agricultural institution. Another one enrolled in a Bible Institute in Manaus.

The efforts which began in a humble way were being rewarded as these young people went on to further studies. Some entered into municipal politics and were elected as councillors.

CHAPTER SEVENTEEN

FURLOUGH - 1956

Every afternoon, after spending the day in language study, I would take the family down to the river for a swim and to wash clothes. Some days the gnats were so bad that we either stayed completely under water or wore clothes for protection. While Betty washed clothes in our port, our daughters and I swam around in the eddies near a huge rock. They all learned to swim at an early age. The girls knew exactly when it was time to go down to the river. Joanne, at three years of age, had noticed that, usually, around four o'clock in the afternoon some clouds formed in a valley on the mountainside across the river. Then she would remind us by saying, "The clouds are coming down."

The girls just loved to eat with the Indians because then they could use their fingers instead of forks. They ate everything put before them. Once we stopped at a village and the girls scampered up to the houses and played with the Indian children while their mother talked with some of the ladies. Soon they brought a small gourd of round, brown things which Betty didn't recognize. She saw the Indian women eating them and had some herself and called the girls to join her. They enjoyed them.

When I joined them, a few minutes later, I saw they were eating *tanajuras*, female leaf cutting ants, loaded with eggs. When I told them what they were eating Betty, immediately stopped but the girls continued to enjoy them.

Audrey, the oldest, quickly gained a good command of the language and interpreted for her mother whenever the Indian women came to trade for soap, thread, needles or other trade goods. She wasn't always quite as helpful though, especially the time when she gave her younger sister Joanne some Epsom salt which she had just tasted herself first. She had a cup of water ready to wash down the bitter salt.

Two years within the tribe had gone very fast. We had come to know the Indians and they had accepted us. Our three daughters, even though they were white with blond hair, had made good friends. We had been in Brazil over four years and began to think of our first furlough. Really, in some ways we would have liked to stay on but we needed to think of our children, Audrey was nearing school age.

We received mission leadership approval to leave a few months early to have our fourth child in Canada. We began to sort our belongings, – some to be packed, others to be given to the lady missionaries or to the Indians. The Indians were not too happy to see us leave. They said they were afraid we would not return because others ahead of us had gone and had not returned. This gave us mixed feelings. We wanted to go on furlough but we did not want to disappoint the Indians. They were putting us to the test; if we returned we would be their true friends if not, then we would be like those who had left them never to return.

Finally it was time to leave the post for a year of furlough. The lady missionaries were staying on to run the post, teach the Indian children and take care of those who would come with whatever illness they might have.

The day came and we were on our way. The canoe was ready with Joaquim as our guide again. We had come to love and appreciate him very much. The girls called him "Baba", Grandfather.

While we were taking our leave in Tunui, Madalena approached Betty and started talking to her. Since Betty wasn't quite sure what she was telling her, she beckoned me from a distance. Madalena was telling her to take the berries she was offering her. She had heard Betty was expecting and she wanted her to have a son. She explained to her that the berries are boy testes and turning to her daughter-in-law, who had three sons, she flipped her baby's testes to emphasize the berries' importance. Betty turned to me and asked, "What shall I do?"

"Just accept them and we'll decide later." I told her.

Later, as we traveled in our canoe on our way down river to Manaus, with only Joaquim with us, I asked him about the berries. He smiled as if he was embarrassed and told me to just dump them in the river. This I did when I was sure he wasn't watching.

On the last day of our canoe trip down the Isana River to catch the amphibious plane to Manaus we stopped at a large village to say farewell. Betty said she would stay down with the canoe and give the girls a swim in the river while I went up into the village. While I was talking to the church leader, I suddenly heard a piercing scream from the river bank and before I knew it, the man I was talking with jumped up and in a flash was down by the canoe. I followed and got to the river bank in time to see him pull Joanne out of the water.

Betty and the girls hadn't realized the rock in the port was slippery until Joanne slipped into the current and was on her way downstream. She was floating past the end of our canoe when the Indian jumped in and grabbed her. She was safe but we were thoroughly shaken up.

Later on Joanne said, "I wasn't afraid when I was under water. I could feel the rock with my feet and pushed myself up, and Jesus had the man save me." The Indians felt very badly about this and told us they knew the rocks were slippery that time of year and they should have told us. Together we thanked God for protecting Joanne.

The next day we arrived at Vila Isana, near the mouth of the Isana River to take the amphibious plane to Manaus. The plane made several stops before arriving in Manaus. The girls looked through the windows and saw the water spray during take-off and landing. They thought that was great! After a few days of paper work and other preparations we took another plane to Belem, at the mouth of the Amazon River. There we boarded the plane for home just before dawn. As we gained altitude in the jet, we wondered what the future held for us. Presently we saw the sun rise out of the Atlantic Ocean.

During the flight to Miami I entered into conversation with an anthropologist sitting next to me. He discovered we had lived with Indians and asked many strange questions. It led to the incident about the berries and he asked if we had kept, at least, one of them. He showed his disappointment when he discovered he had just lost the long-sought-for substance to insure the birth of male babies.

Upon our arrival at the Miami International Airport, my parents met us. They had been waiting to see their two granddaughters who were born after we went to Brazil. The girls loved their grandparents immediately. Soon we got into my parents' car and we were on our way to Canada.

We were driving north on Sunshine Highway in Dad's new Ford when all of a sudden he slowed down to a stop on the shoulder. "It's your turn to drive," he said handing me a new drivers' license which required my signature. It didn't take long for me to discover how much the years of jungle life had changed me. Life was fast. Cars raced along at high speeds. I wanted to drive and yet I was afraid. My father taught me to drive before I ever went to school. It had been five years since I sat behind the wheel of a car. I started driving on the shoulder, slowly gaining speed, and then I turned into the outside lane of the busy highway. My speed was still much too slow. Cars whizzed by on my left and others behind me leaned on their horns. Out of the corner of my eye I saw Dad grinning at me. Slowly I gained speed. We had a very pleasant trip all the way to Canada. Our three girls thoroughly enjoyed themselves. They loved to stop at roadside parks for lunches. Everything was so new to them.

One of the first to visit us, after our arrival, was Susanne Plett's father. He wanted to hear all about his daughter's death in Brazil. He sat there wiping tears from his eyes while I told him the whole story. He said that he knew we had done all we could for her.

Furlough was a hectic time. There were so many supporters wanting to see us. At the same time I felt I needed to help my father on the farm. There was a constant conflict between my desires and our responsibility to our supporters and friends. Some times I arrived late for a supper engagement.

Betty's parents had a small apartment available in their house in town and we moved in and sent Audrey off to school. Winter came and invitations to report on our work kept us busy. Betty received many baby clothes for the little one soon be born. On a cold, stormy night, a few days before Christmas, our first son arrived. We named him Henry James and called him Jimmy. He was a strong and healthy baby.

A few months later Kenneth Johnston, chairman of NTM, invited me to accompany him on a series of meetings he had in western Manitoba. We shared things about our lives and I mentioned to him that, at times, I felt guilty because things were going so well for us. We had a perfect family, we were healthy and happy in the work while so many others had serious problems. Ken turned to me and said, "Your time of trouble is coming, sooner or later, don't rush it."

It wasn't long after that when we heard from Walnie Kliewer, who was keeping our boat and motor at his post near the mouth of the Isana River while we were away. Kenneth Johnston, chairman of NTM International, and several business men, faithful supporters of the Mission had gone to look at the mission work on the Isana River. While there they had used my boat and outboard motor, with Walnie's small motor for a spare, to make a trip up the Isana River to see the work God was doing among the villages. They stopped at a sloping rock for lunch one day and lit a kerosene stove. The boat caught fire and they lost everything. The nearby religious mission helped them. Then they were able to paddle the charred boat downstream again. Later on, these business men sent back two new outboard motors to replace the two destroyed motors.

After the New Year I enrolled in a special Greek language course in the local Bible College and was accepted as a special student. I enjoyed studying and was doing quite well, thanks to a very good instructor.

The local Bible College hosted their spring conference in April, where Betty and I were to give reports. It was also time to get the farm machinery ready for seeding. Dad was very glad for my help and I enjoyed working with him. I even skipped a session or two of the conference and was absent when Betty gave a report on her part of our work in Brazil.

The following day we both prepared to attend the conference. Betty wore a lovely grey dress she had just recently bought. I felt a deep love and gratitude for my wife as I opened the front door of the College. As we went down the short corridor towards the gym where the sessions were held, we walked down a slight decline. Betty turned to me and said, "Henry, I feel faint."

"Let's go back, then," I replied. In an instant she collapsed. I tried to carry her back to the foyer, while somebody helped me. Betty was unconscious! We laid her down on the floor. Somebody called a doctor. The doctor wanted her in the hospital immediately. My Greek teacher said he'd take her. Compassionate hands carried her to the waiting car. With the horn blaring he raced to the hospital.

Orderlies with a stretcher were there waiting at the entrance, ready to whisk her into the emergency room. Our family doctor was there feeling her pulse, ready to pump oxygen into her lungs. "There is no pulse," he informed me. "Do you want me to use oxygen anyway?"

"Yes, try it," I cried in desperation. I saw her chest go up and down with the oxygen, but to no avail.

"Henry, I'm sorry, she is gone," the doctor said, sadly. I stood there, numb, like a stone.

Time seemed to have stopped!

My heart screamed, "My wife is gone! It can't be true!" But it was true. The doctor led me into the nearby lounge and suggested I lie down on the couch.

I couldn't think! My mind was blank! Then I remembered, my wife was gone, leaving me with four children.

Things had been going so well for us. We were all healthy, our girls gave us great joy, and the baby was growing fast. "Lord," I said. "I don't deserve this. Old men lose their wives, I am too young for this." The pain in my heart was ripping it apart. My wife was gone! She had been brutally torn away. I felt frightfully alone, deprived and robbed.

Then the door opened and my father-in-law walked in and sat down next to me. He was quiet for a while before he said anything. "Henry, have you thanked God for this?" He continued, "God gave, now He has taken! Thank Him for it." As much as I loved and respected him I just didn't think he was rational, but I also knew he had gone through the same experience. Why should I thank God for taking my precious wife away so suddenly?

The doctor told me Betty's body had been taken away and I should return to my home. There I found my family waiting for me. They were all in shock. My dear parents didn't have words to comfort me. They clearly remembered their daughter's drowning death ten years earlier. They understood, at least, up to a point. Her death, too, had been so sudden. They ached for me.

Joanne and Arlene were too young to understand but appeared to be sad because everybody else was sad. Martha, my sister, drove out to get Audrey from school. Before long I noticed that Susanne Plett's aging father had come and was sitting there silently, letting me know he sympathized. My sister Annie came to tell me she was taking Jimmy to her place. She had a two-year-old son of her own.

Everybody was concerned and helpful. Even my daughters were a comfort to me. The next day three older gentlemen, well known to the family, came to sit with me. They just wanted to be there for a while, they said. Each one of them had lost his wife. They wanted to be silent support to me. Kenneth Johnston, chairman of New Tribes Mission, was on the train on his way to Prairie Bible College in Alberta to speak at a conference. He got a telegram telling him of Betty's death, and advising him to attend the funeral.

It seemed like time had stopped for me, yet the day of the funeral arrived. It was a cold and blustery April day. The church was packed. Kenneth Johnston preached a sermon. There was some singing but my heart didn't feel like singing. At the end of the service an offering was taken for missions. Then we went to the cemetery. The wind was blowing and sharp snowflakes beat against our faces. There I stood with my three daughters. My parents, Betty's parents, my brother and sisters were all there to support me. Then, Betty's body was lowered into the ground to await the resurrection day. Finally it was time to go. It was too cold to stay any longer and Betty was gone. We had to leave.

Mr. Johnston, driving my car, took me back to the church for a fellowship lunch. My three daughters were in the back seat. With snowflakes bouncing off the windshield, they sat there and began to sing, "Up from the grave He arose. . . " What comfort! What hope!

My daughters were a continual comfort to me. Each one of them reminded me of their mother, as they tried keeping the house in order. They adjusted to the loss of their mother much better than I did. Their faith was strong in God knowing that their mother was in heaven. They were content with having Daddy to take care of them. Their aunts did their best to keep them in good clothes. I was driven to tears watching my sisters and

Betty's sisters do for my daughters what she had done before. I missed her so much!

Then came the lonely days, nights, months! Nothing seemed to have any meaning. I looked out the window and saw cars and trucks on the street and people walking by. Why did their lives continue on when mine had stopped? Didn't they know? Didn't they care?

What was my future? How could I return to Brazil with four children? Who would take over the work I did in Brazil? It was only as I laid all these questions down before God that I received any comfort at all. The Holy Spirit comforted and encouraged me. But, even then, it was unbelievably difficult.

Henry R. Loewen

CHAPTER EIGHTEEN

RETURN TO BRAZIL

My Heavenly Father knew how to create order out of chaos and before I could begin to think of filling the emptiness in my family, He was working. Friends and family were very sympathetic to my particular needs. My sisters and sisters-in-law took good care of my daughters and they had them in their homes frequently, but I preferred to have my daughters at home with me as much was possible. Although my sister Annie took excellent care of Jimmy, I went to see him often to help him remember me as his father. Many times I returned home weeping. I was so lonesome!

I spent much time on my parents' farm, helping Dad with spring seeding and other related jobs. Many evenings I gave reports in various churches about our work in Brazil. I enjoyed doing this but it distressed me very much because it was highly unlikely that I would return to Brazil alone with my four children.

One bleak, lonely day followed another. Weeks and months crept by in slow motion. But God gave healing. He comforted me in my daily fellowship with Him. People everywhere were praying for me.

Remarriage for me was on most people's minds. I knew I couldn't return to Brazil without a wife. Matchmakers had their heyday. I rebelled at such tactics.

If God wanted me to return to Brazil, He would have to get me a wife. I was determined to let Him work this out for me. Nobody was supposed to help me. God directed one of His servants to bring me in contact with the one He had chosen to be my wife and mother of my children.

I was still living in the small apartment in my parents-in-law's place but I didn't spend much of my day there. In the morning I'd get the girls ready for the day and then my mother-in- law took care of them during the day. She said she wanted to do it and the girls loved to spend time with grandma and grandpa.

One day she told me she'd have homemade chicken noodle soup for supper and would like me to join them. That sounded great and I stopped work on the farm early. I always enjoyed her meals and loved to eat with my daughters.

Without telling me she had invited her sister-in-law and two of her daughters. I loved getting to know family better. We had a pleasant time at the table. After supper we retired to the living room.

Edna worked in Nigeria before our marriage.

Edna Reimer, one of my mother-in-law's nieces, was a missionary from Nigeria at home on furlough. We entered into conversation about the differences between the work in Nigeria and Brazil. The conversation became quite animated as she and I continued to discuss the various aspects of the work in both places.

We felt at ease with one another. My mother-in-law's visitors were getting ready to leave but she told them maybe they should wait a little longer so as not to disturb us.

After they left, I thought to myself it had been a good evening. The discussion with Edna about mission work had been like balm to my soul. Here was someone who understood mission work and had a burden to get the Gospel out to needy people. She was the kind of person I would like as a wife and mother of my children. But, I thought, who would want to take on a family of four children?

I continued to help on the farm driving the new diesel farm tractor and doing whatever needed to be done. A heavy weight was slowly lifting off my heart. My daughters were such a comfort to me as we spent time together at home or on the farm with my parents or just taking rides in the car.

Time went on. I thought about the talk I had with Edna and wondered if she would like to talk some more. I needed to go to Winnipeg and invited her to accompany me. She agreed to go with me.

We stopped for pie and coffee at a restaurant. We enjoyed discussing the work each had done on the mission field. We agreed that the evening had been very pleasant and I asked if maybe we could get together again. And, so our friendship grew.

When Edna realized what the implications could be she began to struggle with it. She wanted my friendship but was totally unprepared for the possible consequences. She went to God for direction, guidance and comfort, and received all of it and a confirmation as well.

When we shared our friendship with others in the family they expressed their happiness for us – especially my mother-in-law. As the friendship continued to grow we realized we would need to come to a decision. When we discussed this, both of us agreed we needed to continue seeking God's will for our lives. In due time we agreed we needed each other. We decided to get married. Edna received the peace of God to adopt my four children.

My daughters were thrilled at the prospect of having a mother again. They had been happy the way things were but wanted a stable home again. As time went on we took them along on a few car rides. At first Edna felt strange with the girls but, they accepted her whole-heartedly and made her feel wanted.

Edna had worked with a different mission and belonged to a different church, so we compromised. I would join her church and she would join my mission. Both churches were invited to our wedding. We were missionaries and had many friends who supported us, and we felt we belonged to all of them. The church was full of well-wishers.

My father-in-law set up a fund-raising booth for a boat for us, at the wedding reception. I had previously talked to him, and others, about this need and they wished to give us a long-lasting wedding gift. A substantial amount was raised.

Our honeymoon took us to our mission's headquarters to meet with the leadership. The director received Edna into the fellowship of the mission.

That spring I had rented a field to plant sugar beets. When harvest time came I needed to spend long days, some times way into the night, on the field. Edna was not used to farm life, so had supper ready for me at the usual hour, and being far out on the field, I had no way of letting her know that I was unable to be there on time. She fed the children, then put them to bed and waited for me. I was amazed at her patience and dedication. The profit from the field of sugar beets helped to buy our return passage to Brazil.

When the time came for our departure, the church had an ordination and farewell service for us. It was an ordinary February day, but there was a snowstorm brewing. The meeting went on as scheduled but before long the power went off and we were left in the dark. The ushers scrambled for candles while some hurried off to their homes to get kerosene lamps. Before long, there were candles and lamps burning all over the place and the service continued. Later on refreshments were served with cold water since there was no power for the electric coffee makers. It was a real candle-light farewell service.

CHAPTER NINETEEN

SECOND TERM - 1958

The airport at Belem was shrouded in darkness. It was very hot and humid in the wee hours of the morning when the four-motor DC-10 landed at the airport which lies only a few feet above sea level. Everything looked strange to us but we found our way to the terminal with our hand luggage. We hadn't gone far when we saw Bob Rich waiting for us. Edna didn't know him and the children didn't remember him.

Bob greeted us with enthusiasm and invited us to spend the rest of the night at his place. Our luggage came through customs without incident. The taxi, which Bob had hired, was a tight fit. Then, racing through the empty streets, the driver continually flashed the headlights on and off. We wondered if he were trying to save power, or what? I discovered later on all motorists did that.

Naomi Rich greeted us sleepily and told us she had places prepared for all of us to sleep till daylight. The house was small and there were people sleeping everywhere. Our children felt the heat very much and soon developed prickly heat rash.

We needed to register with the Immigration Office the first thing in the morning. Edna felt so strange in a new country and new language that when she signed her documents she wrote her maiden name. The understanding official said that happened quite often. After she signed her name correctly, we were all registered without further incident. In a few days we took a plane to Manaus.

The flight to Manaus was also during the night, which meant we would arrive in Manaus a few hours before dawn. Macon Hare was there to meet us and told us it really didn't pay to rent a hotel room for the rest of the night. He suggested Edna and the children sleep in hammocks in an upstairs storage room. The room was small, very hot and stuffy with only one small window providing practically no air.

While Edna and the children tried to sleep, Macon and I went downstairs and sat on the steps until morning. We had so much to talk about that time went by quickly. Edna could hardly wait to get out of the sweltering cubicle. At dawn Macon bought some bread and prepared coffee on the one-burner kerosene stove.

Before too long we left for the port where we would take a boat to Puraquequara. The river port in Manaus consisted of dozens of floating shacks where families lived; some had a small store where passersby could buy *guarana*, the authentic Amazon soft drink. Floating walkways connected the houses and stores. The boat which regularly went down river past the Mission headquarters was waiting at the end of one of these floating docks.

As we sat in the boat waiting for it to leave we felt the throb of the one-cylinder engine already running. The children were intrigued by all the refuse on the water. They could see watermelon rind, coconut shells, short pieces of sugarcane, and parts of cheap plastic dolls. There were the dead fish and other refuse that made them pinch their noses. To their amazement they noticed a woman, in one of the floating shacks, dipping water from among the debris with a cooking pot!

Finally, it was time to go. After making a number of stops at other floating-docks, we soon passed the high red-clay cliff on the north side of the Negro River. From there, looking south, we could see the point of land where the Negro River joined the upper Amazon River, which is called Solimões in Brazil, forming the mighty Amazon. The black water of the Negro runs into the murky white water of the Amazon. At first, it looked like black coffee being whitened by cream. The white, muddy water took over slowly, as we moved down river. Before long there was no trace of black water. We were in the Amazon at a point where it is more than ten kilometers wide and meandering along at less than three miles per hour.

Macon Hare pointed out Puraquequara, the New Tribes Mission base. It was a well-kept place. The name, Puraquequara, he told us, meant the place of the electric eel. He said there were several hundred rubber trees and dozens of tall Brazil nut trees on the property. There was a small floating dock where the boat unloaded us. We were among missionaries again.

Everything was strange to Edna after having been in Nigeria for a term; but she adjusted quickly. We were given a comfortable house to live in. The girls loved to swim in the Amazon with other children. They had to be supervised at all times even though they played in shallow water.

Before leaving on furlough two years ago, I had left the Baniwa manuscript of I and II Corinthians to be printed in the mission's print shop. It had not been done because linguists had found some mistakes in it. I spent much time checking and rechecking the manuscript while we were at Puraquequara. Then, after all the corrections had been made, it was ready to be printed.

We also spent much time getting ready to go back up to the Isana River. Edna, being a newly arrived foreigner, had to register with the Federal Police in the State of Amazonas. All this was difficult for her, not knowing any Portuguese at all.

Supplies, for at least two months, had to be purchased and sent on a slow boat to the mouth of the Isana River several months ahead of time.

During that time a decision was made to divide the mission in Brazil into two sectors, the east and west. Each field had to register as such with the local authorities. Macon Hare was the chosen leader in our area along with five others to form the first field committee. New statutes and rules were drawn up and registered with the State government. Since Macon was fairly new in Brazil, I served as his interpreter which gave me many opportunities to learn about government, officials, and much about its legal requirements.

A school for missionaries children would be in operation at the mission base beginning that year, and plans were to have dormitories for the children of those working far away among the tribes. We really anticipated having our oldest two daughters attend school there the coming year. However, we were soon given the disappointing news there would be no room for them in the dormitory but, there might be room for them beginning in January.

That left us with only one option – take them with us to the tribe and home school them. Now we would spend time teaching our girls as well as continuing our ministry.

Several months later, after our supplies had arrived at the mouth of the Isana River we boarded a plane to go to the Baniwa people again. The children were excited about flying in the amphibious plane. Water splashed over the small windows of the plane as it touched the river. There were several stops along the Negro River before we reached Vila Isana where we disembarked.

Clem and Celia Smith, who had been working on the mission station in the mouth of the Isana River, were waiting for us on the huge sand beach. Senhor Fortunato, who was the agent for the airline, invited us into his house for a cup of Brazilian coffee. He told us that while he was storing our supplies in one of his sheds his bull got in there and started to lick on the sugar bag. He had gotten through the burlap material and had licked up some sugar as well. He said he would replace the sugar whenever he was able to do so. After a short visit with our Brazilian friends of Vila Isana we got into the Smith's canoe and began our trip into the Isana River. We hadn't gone very far when Clem pulled the canoe over to a large flat rock near the river bank. "Time for lunch," he called out.

Their two children, Richard and Sherril, were with them. They were helpful in getting the small kerosene stove started and put a pot of beans on. The beans, which were precooked, were soon hot and we began our meal out on the Negro River. There were many cooked weevils which we lined up on the edge of the plates giving it a black border. Edna remarked to Celia about the bugs and was told that there was no way to keep them out. It was either eat or starve.

As soon as we arrived at the mission station at the mouth of the Isana, we began getting ready to continue our trip all the way up to Seringa Ropita, where we had worked before. All our supplies which had previously arrived fit in the large dugout canoe. We got the motor ready which had been in the fire when Kenneth Johnston made a trip with it. The motor had been repaired and was supposed to run well again. As mentioned earlier, the business men who had traveled with Ken had bought two new outboard motors to replace the ones that were burned. I preferred to use my Swedish outboard motor which was much more economical on fuel.

A few days later early in the morning, we began our three-day trip upriver. After several hours of travel, the old Swedish motor began to malfunction. Soon it stopped and wouldn't start gain. About that time a canoe passed by, going down river. We asked the man to take a message to Clem Smith to bring us the five and a half horse power Johnson motor as soon as he could.

In the meantime we paddled into a creek where we stayed overnight with the believers, who gave us a place to hang our hammocks. Since we hadn't seen these people for over two years we had a good time of catching up on the news. They invited me to speak at their evening meeting. Then, early in the morning we went down to our canoe and prepared some corn meal mush sweetened with sugar for our breakfast. The children started to eat and almost simultaneously cried out, "Ugh, this stuff is horrible!"

"Kids," Edna told them finally. "You'll just have to eat it because that is all we have."

"But, Mom, it tastes horrible. You try it." She did and was convinced. The sugar had been tainted with kerosene." They dumped the mush into the creek for the fish and beautiful rings of color showed up where the kerosene floated to the top.

It wasn't long before Clem arrived with the new Johnson motor. While he was there we gave him an order for another bag of sugar to be sent from Manaus. It would be two or maybe three months before it would arrive.

As we made our way upriver we stopped in all the Baniwa villages to greet the believers. Some of the women were so excited to see us again they jumped up and down, crying, "Beh, beh" over and over again. It was such a precious time seeing these dear people again. They were so happy there was somebody there again who could teach them from the Word of God. They gave us bananas and pineapples and smoked fish to show their love to us.

The Tunui mountain was visible several hours before we arrived at the rapids, at the base of the short mountain range. At the Tunui rapids we had to unload all the cargo and carry it over the hill and back to the river. Men, women, and children helped. The women took Edna to a high point above the rapids to watch them pull the dug-out canoe over the rocks. When they were through, everything was put back into the canoe and we began our last lap of the trip.

Seringa Ropita was less than an hour's travel skirting the Tunui mountain. When we came around the last bend, we cheered as we saw our home. Anne Golias and Myrtle Rehn were waiting to greet us. Joaquim and his wife Antonia and their children were waiting too.

Willing hands helped us unload the canoe and carry everything to the house. The lady missionaries had cleaned our house and it was ready for us. It was late in the afternoon and because we were all very tired we prepared a quick supper. Then we put the children to bed. After we prayed with them, Edna and I went outdoors. The full moon was right on top of the mountain with its reflection shimmering in the river. It was Edna's first night at this beautiful spot where we were going to live for God and the Baniwas. While still in Puraquequara, Edna had been teaching second grade to Audrey and kindergarten to Joanne while she herself took classes in Portuguese. Now on the Isana River she taught third grade to Audrey and first to Joanne as well as beginning her ministry among the Baniwa people. Audrey and Joanne responded very well to Edna's teaching, Arlene wanted to learn too, so she started her in the kindergarten lessons.

Audrey, Joanne and Arlene.

There was time before Christmas to take a trip to another river where the people had invited us to teach at their Bible conference. The day we left the weather was perfect as we traveled along the black waters of the Isana River. Finally, we entered into the smaller Aiari River. Here the children looked for flowers and birds as we traveled along. They enjoyed the trip very much.

We had our Zenith Trans Oceanic radio with us to be able to listen to the message service from Manaus every noon. We were expecting a notice from the principal of our school telling us whether or not there would be room for Audrey and Joanne in the dormitory after the first of the year. We also listened to the songs and sermons on radio station HCJB.

It was the time of year when the cormorants migrated. Every afternoon the Indians watched the sky to see them fly over in formation. Around five o'clock the birds began to circle to settle down for the night. The Indians watched carefully to see where they came down to roost.

The men had been preparing darts for their blowguns. Their quivers were full. The older men had been boiling a certain root to make a poison for the tips of the darts. Now they eagerly awaited the slow descent of the birds. They sent out their boys and young men upstream and downstream to find the places where the cormorants would find trees to spend the night. By the time it was dark they were back and reported there were two groups of cormorants in two different locations. Expectation ran very high that evening and it was hard for them to sit and listen to me talk about God's Word. The meeting didn't last very long. They prepared to go out early next morning to bag some of those cormorants while it was still dark.

Noiselessly the men dipped their paddles into the water as one group went downstream and the other upstream. They went as fast as they could in order to reach the trees before dawn. The men shivered in the cool morning air as they waited under the bird-laden branches. No one spoke. They knew what must be done in order to be successful.

When the sky became lighter they could see the outlines of the unsuspecting birds. Slowly, and noiselessly, poisoned darts were slipped into the mouthpiece of each blowgun. They raised them carefully so as not to catch any low-hanging branches.

A puff of breath propelled the darts to their targets. The birds were awakened with a painful start. But they didn't fly away. Their wings were still too wet from dew and it was still too dark. There they perched, not knowing what had happened. Slowly their lungs and other muscles became paralyzed and they dropped noiselessly into the water below. Other darts found their marks and more cormorants fell into the water. By the time the remaining birds became startled and flew away, the canoes were loaded with dozens of birds.

The women were waiting to dress the birds and barbecue them over the fire. They knew that freshly killed cormorants cooked in water have a very strong, wild taste so they always barbecue them. The cormorants were a welcome change after eating only fish for days. Our children loved to eat with the Indians because then they could eat with their fingers, like the Indian children did.

Finally, the day came when we expected a message from the school principal. It came in loud and clear by radio telling us that there would be room for our two girls. We had mixed emotions! We were glad the girls would get a good education, and sad because we would be separated.

The Indians were glad to have us with them. They were happy to learn more about God and the wonderful salvation for the whole world. When we left, they asked us to come back soon because they wanted to know more about God. It had been a pleasure to fellowship with them but it was time to leave the village on the Aiari River and return to our station.

Christmas carols thrilled our hearts on Christmas Eve as we floated down the Isana River towards our home. We could be running the outboard motor, but we wanted to listen to this hour of music over HCJB. Even our Indian guide enjoyed it as he recognized the music of several carols that he knew in his own language.

We looked forward to having duck dinner for our Christmas meal. Some months ago an Indian sold us a duck and we were fattening it for Christmas. But, to our disappointment we found that a hawk had killed it and the woman who looked after our chickens had eaten it rather than let it spoil. We had turtle for our Christmas dinner instead.

I did not prepare the turtle like the Indians used to do. They put the turtle on its back in a big fire. That not only killed it but also roasted the meat making it easier to remove from the shell. Well, when we first saw how they killed turtles, we taught them a lesson in humane killing. We tried to impress upon them turtles have feelings just like people and it was up to us who are more intelligent than animals to treat them fairly and kill them instantly and let out the blood. After that they could roast it within its own shell if they so desired. We told them that Paul wrote a letter to the gentile Christians they should abstain from eating blood and strangled animals. Acts 15:9

That was our Christmas in the jungles of Brazil. The birth of Jesus was just as real to us there as it has been in any other place.

We were careful not to teach any traditions about Christmas to the Indians although we told them what the Church at large did on Christmas

Day. We did not tell them about Santa Claus, the Christmas tree and all the other festivities. We told them December 25 was the day when the birth of Jesus was remembered by Christians as well as by many unbelievers who celebrated it for the sake of festivities.

It would be an understatement to say it was hard to send our children far away to a boarding school even though it was among people we knew well. The girls knew it was best that they go to a school with other missionary children so they made up their minds they would do it even though it was hard. We talked about it together, prayed together about it asking God to watch over them while they were so far away from us.

It worked out just right to have Myrtle Rehn, one of the missionary teachers, accompany them to Manaus, since she needed to go for a medical checkup. The girls loved her.

Edna and I tried our best to be cheerful and be an encouragement to them. When they felt sad about going away so far, we comforted them and directed them to God's constant presence with them.

We had mixed feelings when we saw them board the amphibious plane floating in the water a short distance off the beach at Vila Isana. Soon they are off. The two powerful engines revved up and the float plane gained speed as it passed by sending waves to the beach. We waved at them and committed them entirely into the hands of God, who could keep them much better than we could.

We had much work to do and soon returned to our base. Arlene and Jimmy were good company for each other and a joy to our hearts. Edna taught Arlene but Jimmy wasn't interested in such things. He kept himself busy following his daddy, and asking untold numbers of questions.

Our small canoe, which we named *KOEKATO,* meaning message, was lying on the sloping rock in our river port after having some seams caulked. Near the bow of the canoe were the palm strip mats we used for floor boards. Jimmy stood on those mats to help me push the dugout canoe back into the water. It was really a two man job and he was still quite young so we struggled with it. When I stopped for a short rest I saw, to my horror, he was pinning down a poisonous snake which had been underneath the mats. Its head was out trying to reach the heel of his foot with its deadly fangs. What could I do? If I told him to run the snake would be free to strike him. I couldn't do that! It must have been God telling me to run and snatch him off the mat while I urged him to keep on pushing. I grabbed a nearby machete and the snake lost its head! Jimmy was safe!

CHAPTER TWENTY

CAROL JANE

This following chapter is told by Edna:

When it became evident there would be an addition to our family, we made plans to spend some time in Manaus for the birth of the baby. We waited with much anticipation – maybe, just maybe, there would be a brother for Jim. However, when Carol Jane arrived we were overwhelmed with joy and so glad to have her join our family of three daughters, and one son.

The Isana was no place to give birth to a baby. During our years in Brazil God had directed each step we took. We prepared our boat and left for the three day trip to the mouth of the Isana River where we boarded a Panair plane to the city of Manaus. Going back to a civilized city brought joy and security for me. There was a good doctor and an abundance of vegetables and fruits. There we had a nice apartment where we could relax in comfort. The doctor told me that I was very anemic and needed not only more wholesome food, but I should have a blood transfusion. My pregnancy had been good so far but now I got energy.

I was aroused from a comfortable sleep at about 6 o'clock the 30th of October. Being my first baby, I was not sure if these mild discomforts were for real. No, there were two more weeks to wait. I soon looked at my watch and sure enough, as regular as the clock, contractions came every two minutes. At this point I was ready to go to Santa Casa, the hospital.

It was time for devotions and breakfast. I was not at all in a mood for breakfast. While Henry read a portion from the Bible, I counted nervously as each two minutes passed on my watch. He had breakfast; I sipped coffee and checked the minutes. Lillie Smith, a registered nurse, missionary and friend, was in the mission home with her own one-month old baby. I talked to her through the open window from our upstairs apartment and asked her advice. She remarked that no doubt we had called the doctor and taxi. Really? "Well, get busy!", said she.

In half an hour we called a taxi and were on our way. The contractions were regular, every two minutes. My very close friend, Ruth Allen, who was two weeks late having her baby, had left two hours earlier.

Later we found ourselves in the Santa Casa, the hospital. Arriving at the hospital, Henry asked the nurse if Lillie could be with me during the delivery. "No, that is not allowed," she answered.

Unknown to me Lillie had gotten into a taxi when we were leaving for the hospital. Arriving at Santa Casa I was whisked into the delivery room and told it was time for the baby to arrive. A nurse appeared, took my hand and asked, "Honey, how are you?" Was I in heaven? She spoke English! Lillie found a nurse who gave her a mask and a white uniform and she was in. God was good! Lillie told me that she had left her little baby in care of someone at the mission home for a few hours. However, she advised, if he cries a lot bring him to the hospital since it will soon be the baby's nursing time.

It was less than half an hour later when Carol made her appearance. She was small, six pounds, but was perfect. Ruth my friend had delivered Benny just two hours before Carol arrived. The nurses arranged for us to be in the same room.

Twenty four hours later Henry carried Carol into our apartment at the mission home. Our new baby was dedicated into God's caring hands. Audrey and Joanne arrived from our mission school at Puraquequara for the weekend and together we thanked God for yet another miracle in our family.

Henry was asked to take a trip to the Demeni River with a group of men who took a launch in with supplies. That was fine. Arlene and Jim were good companions and we had missionaries around us. We were happy, but missed Dad.

Carol was colicky, but the doctor examined her and said she was a very healthy baby and would soon settle into a regular routine. And so it was when Henry returned from the Demeni River, we began to make plans to return to our work on the Isana River.

We were busy buying food supplies, including special milk for Carol, and made reservations on Panair. Before leaving Manaus we took Carol for a checkup to the doctor to be sure all was well. We would be in the jungle for months to come.

The time had come for us to leave our comfort zone. We embarked on the 17-passenger float plane to return to our jungle home 1,000 miles from Manaus. After a few hours over the jungle and winding river we noticed the fabric was beginning to tear off the left wing of the plane. The pilot was notified and he returned to a place where the plane could dock in the water near a small village. Little Carol had been sleeping well in the plane. As soon as we got off the plane into the intense heat, she began crying. The hours in the small shelter were very difficult for all of us, especially for Carol. What a relief when we were advised that the plane was now ready to leave, we would be on our way! After a very short time in the air we noticed that the fabric was tearing worse than before. The plane again returned to the same dock. How much more could we take? We returned to the same shelter and waited more hours. More glue came out of the kit, more fabric. Again we prayed that the job would be done well. We wanted safety and we wanted to go home. The afternoon heat became more intolerable, the baby cried more and we prayed. Eventually we were back in the plane and made it safely to the mouth of the river. Thank you God!

Clem and Celia Smith had come to meet the plane. They had waited in this small village for a very long time. They eventually they gave up and started their motor to begin the hour-long trip back to where they lived. Because of the noise of the outboard motor, they did not hear the plane. However, when it got quite close they looked up, and there it was coming in for a landing. What a relief to get into their boat to take us closer to our home! Celia gave us a room where we could stay for a few days just to rest and eat some of her good cooking. Carol, too, was resting from the difficult trip. Soon we all felt much better, ready to start on the last lap of our journey. Unfortunately there were more difficulties ahead.

The river was quite low and we knew this trip would not be easy. There would be rapids to cross, especially Mica Rapids. We said good-bye to the Smiths and proceeded. The weather was favorable while we were traveling, but when the canoe stopped we felt the intense heat, especially when we waited on the large flat rock which was surrounded by angry rapids. We had an umbrella which covered our heads, but oh, it was so painfully hot! Arlene and Jim were with us. We spent some very difficult hours on these extremely hot rocks while Henry and the Indians battled the rapids. Carol cried a lot.

Finally the boat came through the rapids and we were on our way again. The blazing tropical sun beat on us as we went further into the dense jungle area, to our home. The next big rapids were at Tunui. Here we climbed up a very steep hill, and came down on the other side. We were relieved to know that in about thirty-five minutes we would arrive home.

There was one more hurdle. This time we embarked in a much smaller canoe with only a few inches of freeboard and no roof over our heads. Half way to Seringa Ropita, our home, it rained. How much more could we take before our arrival?

But we did arrive. It was so good to be home. We swept the dust and pieces of thatch off the furniture and floor, and worked at getting ready for a new beginning. Henry, always so helpful and thoughtful, worked hard to make everything just right. I must admit I had to again get used to all the bats in the roof, the gnats, the dirt floors, no ceilings etc. I was a bit spoiled after being in Manaus for a few months. Soon the hardships of the trip were forgotten and we began a very special time enjoying the new member of our family. We wished Audrey and Joanne could be there with us to complete our happy family.

Edna and Carol Jane.

Arlene spent many hours with Carol in the hammock, especially when she came down with a cold. Jim enjoyed his time with his Dad in the shop when he was working on the outboard motor.

Carol was sick with a cold a few weeks, but recovered nicely. Henry thought it would be a good time to put new thatch on our house while it was still the dry season. We moved next door into the Stahl's house which they had left when Dorothy suddenly came down with a heart problem. Henry was now doing Bible translation work in that house.

It was during that time Carol had a relapse of her cold and got very sick. I remember how she cried so much, and we felt so very helpless. One night when she had been crying a lot, but finally fallen asleep, Henry and I walked outside to catch some fresh air. The full moon was making sparkles in the ripples on the river flowing past our house. God seemed very close that beautiful, quiet, moonlit night. Suddenly we noticed the night seemed to get darker. We looked at the moon it was not big and round like it was a bit ago. We didn't have the daily paper to tell us when there would be an eclipse of the moon! Soon the moon had disappeared. The night had become dark. Could it be that our baby was slowly being taken from us, just like the moon that night? But still there was hope. However, deep down in my heart I had a feeling she would not be with us much longer.

Our house was now covered with new palm leaves and we could move back. Carol continued to get sicker. We gave her antibiotics. Maybe it was malaria. How could we know? She had a cold, but fever could also be caused by malaria. We could only commit her into God's hands.

One night when while Henry had gone to teach the Indians in the small church in the back of our yard, I stayed home with Carol. She had had a bad day and cried a lot. I had a very small kerosene light in the room, rocking Carol in a wicker rocking chair. At this point we were both crying. I heard the door open quietly and soft footsteps come into the bedroom. It was too dark to see who was there. Without a word the Indian woman took my baby out of my arms, carried her around for a while, then laid her back in my arms. I knew she sorrowed with me. She prayed for Carol and left. No, she had no words. To me she was an angel from God to comfort and encourage me that dark night.

The Indians were planning a Bible conference in a village just an hour upriver. I knew I could not go while Carol was still sick. I had a very strong premonition she would not be with us much longer. Henry felt the same way, but we did not really talk about it. I did not want to keep him from going to the conference. Maybe Carol would improve shortly. The Indians from Tunui came by in their dugout canoes. Some passed on to their destination. Others stopped to see if we were soon going too. A dear old lady, Dona Madalena, came into the house with some of her friends. She immediately noticed Carol was a very sick baby. She looked around at the women standing by. Madalena offered to pray for the baby and anyone who was not willing to pray with her, to leave the house. They all stayed. I was sitting by the table with Carol in my arms. Madalena knelt on the dirt floor beside me, put her hands on Carol's head. She prayed for healing, but for God's will be done. Madalena had a sickness which made her skin rough and black. But to us she had always been a beautiful woman inside. She loved God very much and always was an encouragement to me. After prayer the women left the house and were on their way to conference.

That night was extremely dark. Carol's fever steadily went up. She cried a lot. We put her in her crib, covered her with a thin blanket so we could get some steam to her. By now it was evident she had come down with pneumonia. Henry gently picked her up out of the crib and held her very close. He knew and I knew, that the end was very near. Her breathing was very slow and soon she was gone. Henry laid her on the pillow in our bed. The room was so quiet that dark night. We felt so alone, so far away from family and friends. We went to the other room looking at her through the open door. We noticed how very peaceful she looked. Henry said, "We don't see them, but the angels are in the process of taking her HOME." He said this because when Carol was breathing her last, she opened her big, brown eyes. The she lifted both arms, looking to a point high on the wall she burst into a beautiful smile. He thought she was seeing the angels coming to receive her. We felt relief. She was not crying. She was in the arms of Jesus.

An Indian couple was staying in a shelter some fifty yards away. The man was building a larger boat for us. Early in the morning they both came to our door. They knew Carol was gone since she didn't cry any more. He offered to make a box so we could bury her. We lined the coffin with baby's blankets into the box and gently put her into the coffin. We knew Carol was no longer that body. She was with God. Together with Arlene, Jim, Elizabeth, and the Indian couple, we walked to the edge of the jungle where Raimundo had dug a hole for the coffin. We sang "*In the Sweet Bye and Bye*" and lowered her into the ground in the shade of a white birch tree. We knew God was there with us, even though we felt very much alone. Most of all we missed not having Audrey and Joanne with us. They were at school, a thousand miles away. We felt so bad that they had not been able to spend those short months with their baby sister. Arlene and Jim missed her. He was almost three years old, and did not quite understand all that was happening. He was concerned that Carol had gone without a suitcase with clothes and diapers! Life went on and so did our work with the Indians. Psalm 46:1, 2, God is our refuge and strength, an ever present help in trouble. Therefore we will not fear. Underneath are His everlasting arms.

We wrote a letter to send to our church:

Isana River, April 20, 1960

Job said long ago that God had given him his children and that He had taken them away too. Job 1:21. We felt what Job felt when he saw his children taken away. God removed from our midst our little daughter.

Carol Jane was born a normal, healthy child on October 30, 1959. She was a very special blessing in our home. Her first few months were spent in Manaus suffering the heat. Many times she was just wet with perspiration! We consulted a child specialist and he gave her a special formula on which she did very well.

By the beginning of February we felt that we ought to return to our work. So, we returned to the Isana River again – to our home. The plane trip was none too pleasant. It was very choppy. When we reached altitude it was cool in the plane and whenever we landed on the various stops the heat almost choked us.

Immediately upon our return we noticed Carol was much happier because it was cooler. She ate better and slept better too. This caused us much joy. We stayed with the Smiths for five days just getting rested up.

The river was very low at that time but we had to go to our station. We feared that it would go down much more yet and make it more difficult than ever. So we went. God gave us good weather till we were almost home. We had to cross five big rapids on that trip. It was exceedingly hard for both Baby and Mother to wait on the rocks while the men pulled the boat through and portaged the cargo. God, however, gave strength. At the last rapids we changed boats and motors. This boat had no roof over it. We were only 50 minutes from home so we did not bother to make a shelter. We had no rain till about five minutes before we reached home. We covered Carol well but still it must have been too damp and cool for her.

Two weeks later she became ill with what we think was pneumonia. We gave her several penicillin shots and she recovered in about a week. After she was well, she gained weight real fast and became quite chubby and cuddly. She was such a joy to us for the next three weeks! Like all parents, we were looking into the future. But it was short lived. On Sunday, April 10, we took her to the church service in the morning. Before it was over she began to cry much so we took her home. She became sick again. We gave her penicillin fearing she might have pneumonia again. She got worse. We sat up with her at nights. It was conference time and Henry needed to go, but he stayed, hoping that if in a few days there would be an improvement he would then go to the Indian conference. On Good Friday night we were prepared to stay awake all night again. Our darling became worse. She had spasms when she just threw herself and turned blue. We feared the end was near. She was constantly suffering. At two o'clock in the morning of the sixteenth she breathed her last painful breath.

After her suffering was over, her little face just relaxed and we realized her small body must have suffered very much. We knew she was going, yet it was nigh impossible to believe. We knew God was near and yet He seemed so far. We knew our little one had gone to be with the Savior and yet it pained us so much to see her taken away in such a painful way. We tried to pray but words were gone. We knew God understood. He has comforted our hearts a lot but the vacancy in our home is still there. Oh, how big a place she filled! We shall not again see her lips spread into a beautiful smile, nor will her big dark eyes sparkle with contentment. These are but memories now! But praise God, one day we shall see her in the Savior's presence. "Let the children come to me, do not hinder them; for to such belongs the kingdom of God." Mark 10:14 RSV.

Attending Carol's funeral were Elizabeth Koop and a Baniwa family who was here working for us. The man kindly offered to make a small coffin. Audrey and Joanne were still at school away from home. We gathered in our home and sang a few Portuguese hymns. Henry read some comforting verses in Baniwa. After prayer by this Christian Indian, our daughter was laid to rest – forever safe in the arms of Jesus.

These last few days we have been thinking of a number of you who have gone through what we just experienced. Especially did we remember Leonard Reimers and Gladstone Penners. We just ask one thing of you now and that is to pray. You know the vacancy a child can leave, so do pray that we here in the jungles will lean heavily upon God.

Thank you again for your constant prayers. May God bless you.

Your missionaries,

Henry, Edna and children

CHAPTER TWENTY-ONE

MORE ACCUSATIONS - 1961

The fabrication of more accusations against us did not stop. The perpetrators just sent their allegations to a different department of the government. Before too long the local officers of the State Police asked us leading questions about our work. We offered to take them to the Baniwa and Nyengatu people and see it for themselves. They weren't quite that interested.

Later, after Jim and Skip Curtis had joined the team on the Isana River, Jim and I went to see the chief of the State Police in the city of Manaus.

The police chief was very cordial and listened to us as we explained the reason for working with the Indians on the Isana River. We told him about the high rate of literacy among them and the change in the people's lives after they had embraced the Gospel. We also told him about the accusations that had been directed at us by the adversaries of the Gospel.

"Oh yes", he told us. "I know all about those allegations but have considered them to be rather trivial."

"We're also being accused of looking for gold on the mountain near Tunui," we told him.

"Oh yes," he agreed in good English. "You men are, in fact, looking for gold, but you are looking for human gold." How our hearts rejoiced at his insight into our ministry! He seemed to know we were concerned for the spiritual welfare of the Indians and not in any gain for ourselves. He encouraged us to continue our ministry among the tribal people and to be careful not to irritate our antagonists. He told us he would take care of any further accusations.

Then the perpetrators of these charges turned to the federal army to unload their accusations. They hadn't received the desired attention from the SPI nor from the State Police, so surely the military leaders would be alarmed at the presence of the despicable evangelicals right on the border of Brazil and Colombia!

They took note all right. The army general in Manaus dispatched an order to the lieutenant in command of the border detachment of the area, to investigate the allegations against us.

Bible conference was coming soon to Peach Palm Village and the Indians were preparing for the event with great anticipation. Every morning before breakfast they met for prayer asking God to watch over them as they went to get the needed materials. They rejoiced because their sins were forgiven and they were free from the evil that used to control them. Now they worked hard to prepare their village for a time of fellowship with other believers in Christ from many different villages. Many had gone to work in far away places to earn money for clothes, pots, pans, ammunition and fishing material. They were especially eager to get kerosene for their lamps for the evening services. Everyone, young and old, applied himself to make this the best conference ever.

The best hunters had gone deep into the jungles to hunt for wild pigs, deer, tapir and monkey. Temporary palm huts for visitors went up near the individual homes. A large building, to serve as the meeting place and dining hall, was being built in the center of the village. They wanted a new building to hear God's Word and have their meals.

The village chief sent several men to go to a distant part of the jungle to get palm leaves for the roof. Some cut the poles for the framework. Women and boys pulled down a supply of liana – a vine which hangs down from tall trees – to tie the poles together and to hold down the palm leaves on the roof.

The elders sent out written notes to the leaders of the churches inviting them to arrive in Peach Palm Village the last Tuesday of the month. Their meetings were to begin the following day, and continue for five days, the last day being Sunday.

They wanted the conference to be honoring to their God and Savior. Every evening the elders encouraged the believers from the Word of God to a closer walk with God and to be strong in the faith. They exhorted the women to watch themselves and not become involved in gossip when their friends would arrive from other villages.

The children had spent much time trying to learn to read and write in their own language. Some also had studied Portuguese. Myrtle Rehn and Elizabeth Koop, who lived on our station, had been in this village to help the Baniwas to learn to read and write. The youngsters had really applied themselves and were progressing well in both reading and writing. In their spare time they helped their parents to get ready for the conference. They took off in their small canoes up the tributaries for fish, or they went into the woods to shoot birds with their blowguns.

A week before the conference they were all together admiring the large, new building and the smaller shelters for visitors. All that remained to be done was to clean the yard and cut the reeds on the riverbank where they would welcome the visitors. The chief was satisfied with all the workers.

Edna and I, Elizabeth and Myrtle were looking forward to a great time of fellowship with the Baniwa and a few Curipaco believers. We planned to leave for Peach Palm Village several days before the meetings were to begin, and planned to stop in every village on the way. The believers needed encouragement and there were many who still did not believe in Jesus.

Antonio, a strong believer in Jesus, who loved to teach, was our guide on this trip. Unfortunately, his wife Antonia and small child had to stay at our place because there was no more room in the canoe. Edna and Jimmy were along too. Arlene had by this time joined her two sisters at the boarding school. With the four of us the boat was loaded to capacity.

In one village they asked for medicine to get rid of parasites. Several in the village where we spent the night had black blotches on their skin and wanted injections to cure it. Fortunately, we still had some of the medicine the department of health had supplied.

We had a long distance to travel, so at break of dawn we were on our way upstream again. Antonio, our guide, knew of a sand beach where we could cook some tapioca for breakfast. He loved to travel with us and tried to accommodate us in our foreign ways. He watched us closely to see how we acted as believers in Christ. At Barcelos, a small village, all the men were out hunting. The two remaining women were anxious to be treated for the skin blotch disease, so I gave them each an injection. Then they gave me two muzzle loader guns, which their owners had left for me to repair, which I did.

Farther along the way we stopped at two more villages where we traded some fresh and smoked fish for ammunition. Just before nightfall we reached a very high sand bank called Frog Point. Antonio gathered dry wood to start a fire. Then he went to get green poles to dig into the damp sand to hang our hammocks. Darkness comes quickly in the jungles right on the equator. By the time our meal was ready, the full moon gave us sufficient light for eating. Antonio made sure there was plenty of firewood and we lay down to sleep. Lying in the hammocks, we talked about the Lord Jesus and His teaching for a while.

Antonio was checking the sand carefully when I awoke early next morning. "Did you lose something?" I asked him.

"No," he replied with concern, "I'm looking at the jaguar tracks in the sand. It looks like we had a full-grown jaguar visiting us last night."

Jaguars are known to take children out of their hammocks.

"Really, Antonio, God watches over His own, doesn't He?"

"Yes, Ariki, He even controls the jaguars."

Antonio knew only too well that jaguars frequently take children from their hammocks. We were reminded of the verse in I Peter 5:8, which warns us to: Be sober, be vigilant; because your adversary the devil, as a roaring lion, walks about, seeking whom he may devour. After breakfast we were on our way again. Antonio was quite happy operating the outboard motor rather than paddling slowly against the current.

A few bends later we stopped at a small place with two palm leaf shelters. The people had sore eyes and asked for treatment. We had antibiotic eye ointment in our kit and gave them a small tube. Out of gratitude, they gave us some fish. We were so thankful this ointment had arrived in time for this trip because there were so many with sore eyes. It was strange they wanted this ointment when they knew the sap of a certain vine was good for sore eyes. We have used it successfully ourselves.

Soon we arrived at a huge, flat, sand beach. There were a number of families camping out and getting ready to go to the meetings at Peach Palm Village. As was their custom, they gave us some smoked birds. They were full of enthusiasm about the meetings in the next village.

Baniwas arriving at conference.

By the time we arrived at Peach Palm Village the sun was directly overhead. The people had heard the sound of our outboard motor for some time and were waiting for us at the riverbank singing welcome songs for us in their own language. As was their custom they expected me and our four-year-old son Jimmy, to go up the line of people first and then Edna, greeting each person separately. Each one of them greeted us with hefty handshakes saying, "You have arrived", or "I'm happy to see you". They also patted me and Jimmy on the shoulder showing their satisfaction in seeing us.

Like an army of ants, they got on our boat and began handing our baggage to those on the bank to be carried to the chapel where we were to stay. Everything was left in place in a corner of the room. It would have taken Antonio and me a long time to carry all our stuff the long distance from the river. By that time all the folks from nearby villages had arrived and were assigned a place to sleep. The place was crawling with people. Everyone was excited to meet those they hadn't seen for some time.

True to their culture it didn't take long before they had a meal ready for all of us. The special of the day was dried fish soup. There were huge stacks of smoked meat but all that was reserved for the conference which really began only the next day. The soup was delicious!

At the clanging of an improvised bell, a gathering was announced for the afternoon. Immediately women scurried around trying to find their children to take them to the meeting. The men sauntered towards the large, new building in which were row upon row of newly axe-hewn logs to serve as benches. The walls were only thin poles set close together to permit the breezes to blow through and to keep dogs out. In a short while the benches were almost full. The church leaders called the meeting to order by starting songs and choruses. How they sang with their untrained voices, but they meant what they sang. Surely God must have been pleased with their songs of praise and worship.

All the men of the host village sat on raised log platforms facing the crowd. Later they would give their testimonies to share their faith in Jesus. The church leader, who was the chairman, stood up as he led in prayer, his hands covering his face. Then the women and young girls of the host village made their way to the front and began giving their testimonies, one by one.

The chief's wife was a vibrant believer. Ever since she had trusted Jesus to take away her sins she overflowed with happiness. All her fears were gone and she looked forward to living with Jesus up in heaven after this life was over. She prayed for her children every morning. Her heart was very glad that all the people had come to her village to hear more about God.

The main part of most testimonies was their faith in Jesus Christ. Some mentioned how they had struggled before they placed their faith in the living Son of God. Many of them told how they first heard the Word of God and when they learned to read the Word they decided to place their faith in Jesus. Most of them mentioned that Jesus had taken away their fear. Some honestly talked about the battles they faced now that they were believers in Christ. The children got their turn to sing a few songs and recite some Bible verses. Some of them knew many verses. A few were bashful and fidgety but they did their part to make the meeting a success.

Finally the men got their turn. Each one stood up on the raised platform at the front, prayed with his hands covering his face, read a portion from the New Testament and proceeded to give his testimony. Some had a very clear understanding of salvation by grace, others were struggling in their faith, trying to hold on to it by good works. They had the same battle believers all over the world have. The enemy makes them doubt salvation by grace and they try to earn salvation by works. There definitely was need for more Bible teaching.

After the last testimony they asked me to teach them but I decided to answer any of their questions. Many referred to verses they didn't understand. The rest of the afternoon was spent answering questions and sorting out their problems.

It was dusk when we heard the sound of an outboard motor.

"Who could be coming to see us this late in the day?" they asked one another.

One of the older men said, "Nobody travels this river by night with all the rocks in it. Who could be so desperate?"

"I hope they bring us good news from the outside world," was another comment. Many of the Indians ran to the river bank to meet the strangers who came to their village in a boat with a powerful outboard motor. Later they told me the men were traders and wanted to buy otter skins.

"They must be very ignorant because everybody knows the otters in this part of the river are of very poor quality," said one of the young men.

During the evening meeting I taught them in Baniwa from Philippians 2:1-2 about practicing unity and love in the strength of the Holy Spirit. Everyone appeared to be listening attentively while we smelled cigarette smoke from the traders. It seemed strange to me the traders would travel all that distance in a high powered outboard motor boat just to buy otter skins.

There was a heavy fog enveloping the whole village in the early hours of the morning. Dampness crept in everywhere. The sound of singing a wake-up song by church leaders filtered through the cool stillness to arouse the believers for prayer meeting. Others joined in escalating volume and it became a scattered choir from dozens of hammocks. The leader led in a short prayer, from his hammock, then many came to the small chapel where we were billeted. Earnest prayers went up to our Father God in heaven imploring Him to bless our time together during the day and to protect each one from harm and evil. We were unaware of the evil intentions of the visitors of the previous night.

Henry R. Loewen

CHAPTER TWENTY-TWO

ARRESTED BY ARMY

The thick mist had barely enveloped the last person leaving the chapel when a dark shadow appeared in the doorway making its way toward me. Ignoring Edna's presence, he began speaking to me in an agitated manner. I couldn't understand him so I asked him to please speak in Portuguese because I did not speak Spanish.

In a slower but still tense voice he said, "I am Lieutenant Licciardi from the army base at Cucui. I have been sent here to take you away. You are now prisoners. And I am speaking in Portuguese."

"Where are you taking us?"

"To Boa Vista, where Walnie and Jim are," he replied.

Boa Vista was at the mouth of the Isana River. There was an Indian village as well as a mission station located there.

"Would you please show me your orders to take me away from my work here?" I said.

Reluctantly he showed me his military identification card, I repeated my request.

"Please show me the written order to take me away."

"I follow an oral order," he replied.

"Who gave you this order?" I asked.

"My General in Manaus. The one who is in charge of all boundary territory."

He ordered me very abruptly not to speak anything in Baniwa from then on and commanded me to get our things together and get ready to go.

"Look, my young son is lying asleep here in his hammock. Do you want me to awaken him at this early hour?"

"Awaken him," he ordered.

"May we have breakfast before we go?" I asked.

"No, we'll have breakfast on board the boat."

While the officer was watching, I awakened Jimmy from a sound sleep and took him to greet the soldier. Of course, he did not know what was going on and sleepily held out his hand to greet him.

As I took Jimmy along the path into the woods, I prayed.

"God, I don't know what is going on. I need your guidance and your wisdom. What shall we do? Shall we resist and demand our rights to remain, or shall we quietly accompany the officer?"

God quietly brought to my mind that we were to obey those in authority.

"Okay, God. We will go with him and leave the future in your hands."

The officer was waiting for me and told me we might as well have our breakfast before leaving, but I told him we'd just go.

"Tell the other two women to get ready to go too," he ordered me, referring to Elizabeth Koop and Myrtle Rehn who had been teaching there in the village. After explaining to the two ladies what was going on, I addressed the lieutenant again. "Would you please tell the Indians why you are taking us away?"

"No, you tell them," he rebutted. He ordered one of the men he had along to interpret into Baniwa since I was forbidden to talk in their language.

Addressing the Baniwa men I said, "This man is an officer of the Brazilian army and is taking all of us away. The Bible teaches us to obey those in authority. I want you all to pray much to God for us so we will be able to return soon and we will always pray for you."

Edna and I got our things together, and the dear, concerned Christian Indians, carried our baggage down to the boat. Soon we were ready to leave. And all the people were quietly standing in tangible silence on the grassy bank wondering what was going to happen to us.

The lieutenant was on shore with his crew, except for one who was ready at the motor. He was quite anxious to get going.

We had taught the Indians to commit themselves to God's protection before any trips. We needed it especially now, not knowing what lay ahead. We needed God's protection more than ever. Standing on the bow of our boat, while Antonio was at the motor, I addressed the officer.

"Lieutenant, it is our custom to commit our ways to our God before we travel and we are going to do so right now." I saw the Indians on the bank covering their faces with their hands to join with me while I prayed in Portuguese, for the benefit of the officer. "Our Heavenly Father, we commit ourselves to your care and protection as we begin this trip. We do not know what lies ahead, but you do and we thank you for it. I pray also that the lieutenant and his men will travel safely and that they all come to know you personally. Watch over these dear people who are staying here. In Jesus' name. Amen."

The lieutenant commanded me to go ahead and he would follow. So, at seven in the morning instead of joining the Baniwas for breakfast and the fellowship meetings we were on our way down river. Elizabeth and Myrtle followed us in their canoe. We were not moving fast with only a 6 horse-power Johnson motor pushing our canoe. The lieutenant followed us at the same speed till about eleven o'clock when he went on ahead and stopped at the next deserted village.

As we approached, we saw the men sharpening their machetes on the sandstone lying in the rocky port. Edna thought that surely they had evil intentions towards us. We stopped to talk to them and saw they were killing a turtle for their lunch. The lieutenant told us we could go on ahead to our station.

We gladly moved on to get out of their presence. The lieutenant was not honest with us and he certainly was not friendly. We kept on talking among ourselves about the possible reason for the detention. What had we done wrong that merited the army removing us from our work? We had valid SPI permits to work among the Indians on this river. What could be the reason?

We remembered the Indians had been telling us the religious leader repeatedly told them that soon the missionaries would be removed from this river never to return. We recalled the time when there was a four-page letter of accusations against us by the religious leader, and the SPI agent had asked me to meet him urgently to justify ourselves. Could this be a continuation of the same accusations?

At Pineapple Village we let off the guide who was traveling with the ladies. The lieutenant had not caught up with us to that point and at five o'clock we arrived at Seringa Ropita, our home.

Laura, the woman we had left in charge, greeted us down at the riverbank and immediately asked us why we had returned so soon. We told her briefly, and she became very agitated. She told us that the same men had stopped and talked to her the previous day. They had passed our place and stopped at the next village, then turned around and came back to Seringa Ropita.

The officer had questioned Laura on just about every subject while her husband was out fishing.

"Do you have food to eat?"

"Are you watching the place?"

"Do they pay you?"

When Raimundo, her husband arrived, they asked him a lot of questions too.

"Why don't the missionaries plant corn and other things on the station?"

"Why don't they raise pigs and chickens?"

"Do the missionaries feed you?"

"Why don't you buy at the other religious mission?"

The lieutenant had asked for the key to get into our house. There was no key so he forced the door open with a screw driver. He went in and looked over everything, making obscene remarks about us. Raimundo, Laura's husband who had just arrived, knowing Portuguese understood everything. Then he took a box full of canned goods out of the house and gave it to the Indians to eat. They did not want to receive it for themselves, but figured it would be better to take it for the sake of peace.

He demanded the key to the other vacant house and entered it. There too he searched everything. That house was used for Bible translation and printing. He took three cans of gasoline which belonged to a Colombian trader who had left it some time ago.

The lieutenant arrived while we were still standing beside the river. We knew he did not go to the Cuiari River like he told us he would. He did not waste any time to tell us that we could stay overnight in our house but should be at Tunui, the next village down river, by 9:00 am, where he would wait for us.

"We'd like you to stay overnight with us and have a good supper here."

He declined the invitation with a shame-faced look on his sun-burned face. I offered him some ointment for the painful blisters and bleeding lips, but he declined it. Turning around to go on his way he called back reminding us to be at Tunui at nine in the morning. We were still puzzled.

What was all this about? What had we done to provoke the authorities? But there was no point in wondering now. We had our orders to get ready to leave.

"Edna, let's leave our things where they won't suffer if we stay a long time. I will put insect poison around every thing the ants might want to eat."

She said, "I'll put all the linens and blankets in drawers." All our extra groceries were put into large tin cans and placed in the attic." The house was in order, as much as possible, in a short time. We wondered what to take along and what to leave. Edna's accordion was placed on the upper bunk in the bedroom and covered with a blanket. The window shutters were well secured and nothing perishable was left anywhere. Raimundo and Laura offered to watch our place. They were very sad but understood that we had no choice.

We decided to take as much as possible in the canoe to take to the station at the mouth of the river. Everything was loaded into a borrowed canoe which Antonio and his wife paddled down to Tunui. There the Indians would help carry everything across to the lower side of the rapids into our larger canoe that was tied up there. We suggested to Antonio that he keep his ears and eyes open to what the officer and soldiers would say and do at night. By dusk they were floating downstream towards the roaring rapids at Tunui.

At a prayer meeting that night we committed our uncertain future to God. He gave us peace in our hearts. Raimundo and Laura joined the four of us, on our knees, as we praised God for His indwelling presence and His sure promise to be with us at all times.

Antonio told me later that the officer told the Indians at Tunui he'd see them in their village after a while to talk with them. When he saw me arriving with your baggage, he and his men remained down at the riverbank. They seemed to be afraid of us. The soldiers bought a chicken for their supper but the officer did not go to visit with them as he had promised. Antonio went on to say, "I was listening from a hidden place to hear them talk. They were fearful of what the Indians might do to them at night." After some silence Antonio said, "The lieutenant and his soldiers do not know that since the Lord Jesus entered our lives, we would rather defend than harm them. They had one soldier standing guard during the night hours.

Arriving at Tunui more than an hour sooner than we had been ordered, the Indians immediately helped us carry our belongings to the lower side of the rapids. We were ready to leave long before the officer. We gave the Indians a five gallon can of kerosene for their help in crossing the rapids. They were deeply concerned for us and promised always to pray for our soon return. They told us they believed God would bring us back. Maybe their faith was stronger than ours.

I climbed the steep rocky path back up to the village to tell the officer that we were ready to go and asked him if we could go on ahead of him.

"No, I want you to wait for us because we are going to use our smaller motor," he replied. He returned the three cans of gasoline he took from our station on his way up river to get us. Nevertheless, we began drifting down river with the current while we waited for them to catch up with us. It wasn't until nearly ten o'clock that we saw them coming in their boat. It was soon evident that the soldiers were traveling much faster than we could with our larger, heavily loaded boat. So, they passed us and went on ahead till we saw them cooking their lunch on the rocky port of a village. We kept on going to the next village where our guide lived.

Antonio was willing to accompany us all the way but would leave his wife and child at home. He hurriedly packed a clean hammock and clothes, while he told his people why he was taking us. They were deeply troubled by our sudden departure and, especially the women were greatly alarmed as they remembered how Sophie Muller was taken into custody by government authorities some years ago. The believers promised to keep on praying that we would soon return.

Several fellows offered to help us pass Mica Rapids, just a short distance from their village. These rapids were of the most treacherous on the Isana River. With every level of the water the channel was different. The Indians had lived here all their lives and knew where the channels were, even at night. They took us safely through narrow gorges between threatening rocks. They appeared to be enjoying it, but our knuckles were white from grasping the edge of the boat. Then, suddenly we were in quiet waters again.

By this time we wished we could get far ahead of the officer who arrested us. We suggested to the Indians not to hurry when they would help the lieutenant through the rapids. We were hoping that we would be able to reach Boa Vista ahead of our captor, lest he force us to stay overnight at the religious mission on the way to the mouth of the Isana River.

Antonio kept the boat going downstream at a steady speed in the swiftest part of the river. He had much less of a desire to stay overnight at the religious mission. He and his family had been shying away from them ever since they took their brother out of the religious mission school soon after the family became believers.

We kept on looking back to see if the lieutenant was gaining on us. Soon there were just a few bends in the river before we would pass the religious mission station and still the officer was not in sight. As we passed by the mission, in the middle of the river, we noticed the religious leader was pacing back and forth on the grassy riverbank. There were several adults and a group of children with him. He appeared to be frustrated when he noticed the officer wasn't with us and we were passing by. We waved at him but he didn't respond. We kept on going. We discussed the religious leader's frustrated pacing and refusal to respond to our waving, and wondered if he was aware of the officer's mission and if he was, somehow, involved.

CHAPTER TWENTY-THREE

MORE ARRESTS

The six horse power motor just kept on purring along as we made our way toward the mouth of the Isana River. We had about one hour of daylight left and about four hours to travel.

We wondered if the officer would stay overnight with the religious leader. With all the anxiety and tension of the day we suddenly felt hungry so we stopped at the nearest sand bar at Fire Ant Point to have something to eat before it was completely dark. We had some food of our own, and plenty of smoked fish the believers had given us as a love offering. We thanked God for the food and for His protection. After refilling the gas tank, we were on our way again, still wondering what was happening with our captors.

It was midnight when we arrived at Boa Vista, at the mouth of the Isana River. Nobody came to meet us at the port. The Indians always came to greet whoever might come, at any time of day. We wondered why they didn't show up now. Tying up the boat we took some of our baggage up to the houses. In the darkness we could see the shutters on Curtis' house were closed. That meant they were not home. There was a guest house to which Myrtle had a key and she let us in. We could all spend the night there.

I needed to know where the missionaries were and went to the nearby village to ask. Of course the Indians were awake. Their dogs had been barking ever since we arrived. Chief Julio Americo came out of his house to see who was there. He was relieved when he saw me. Soon others appeared.

"Where are Jim and Skip and Walnie?" I enquired.

"Ariki, they went to teach on the Cubate River," the chief answered. Then I asked them what they knew about an army lieutenant going up river to get us. Of course they knew nothing about an army officer.

"But," they told me, "a man with six others had stopped a few days ago. He told us that he was going to Tunui to get rubber and wood."

"We thought he was lying to us because everybody knows there are no rubber trees near Tunui. Now we know he was lying." It appeared he never mentioned anything to Jim and Walnie or they would not have gone up river to teach.

Sunday morning we still wondered what might happen when the lieutenant would arrive. After breakfast Antonio trimmed my hair and we joined the Nyengatu believers in their worship service. The leader had asked Antonio, who knew the Nyengatu language well, to preach.

He chose Matthew 5:1-12, dwelling more on the last two verses. He told the believers, "God's Word tells us that we are blessed when people persecute us and speak all kinds of evil against us falsely because of Christ. It also tells us that we must rejoice and be very glad because there is a reward for us in heaven."

I wondered if Antonio had been thinking about that while he operated our motor all the way down river. It was a very timely message from one of God's chosen servants.

One of the older men invited us to have lunch with him in his house. We accepted gladly and appreciated their warm fellowship. We felt we were not alone any more. All of the believers sympathized with us and wondered what was going to happen.

The sun was beginning to drop toward the horizon when the lieutenant and his men arrived. We watched from the house and saw him come striding up the path as if he owned the place.

When he saw the Curtis' house was closed up he barked at me.

"Where are the Curtises? "

"Sir, they have gone up the Cubate River to teach," I told him.

"Where are the Curtises?" he loudly repeated the question.

"Sir," I repeated. "They all went up the Cubate River to teach."

The Indian women standing near us were so frightened at the fury of the officer, they wanted to hide in our house. We suggested they be calm and cooperate.

Approaching us, the lieutenant asked me how far it was to where the Curtises and Walnie went and ordered his soldiers to come up to him. Promptly they arrived with machine-guns in their sacks.

"Go into the Indian village and search it for the other missionaries," he commanded them.

Turning to us he barked, "You are all prisoners and your chief will be prisoner too." Then he demanded all our documents – passports and personal Brazilian identification cards. What could we do but to comply, even though we knew it was unlawful for him to take our documents.

They left for the Cubate River and I hurried down to our launch which had been tied up while we were farther upriver. I was glad nobody had harmed it or even taken it while we were at the conference. By evening it was ready for traveling.

We felt it was important we write down everything that had happened so far and leave it with one of the Indians to give to somebody who would know what to do with it.

Myrtle Rehn wrote to Bob Rich in Manaus:

LORD, ALLOW THIS LETTER TO REACH BOB RICH!

Dear Bob,

This is an <u>urgent</u> letter for prayer and help, but our God is Almighty and <u>above</u> all powers in heaven and earth.

Henry, Edna, Jimmy, Elizabeth and I are being taken <u>prisoners</u> to Cucui! They (the soldiers) are going to get Jim, Skip and family now, also Walnie, and no doubt David Sharp. It just happened that our folk here went up on the Cubate on Friday so were not here when we arrived here about 12:30 after mid-night.

Elizabeth and I were way up on the Isana River at a conference at Peach Palm Village, just above the mouth of the Aiari River but on the Isana River. On the second day of the conference about noon, Jan. 26th, Henry, Edna and Jimmy arrived. Just as the evening meeting was starting, a motor arrived, but we saw no sign of the ones who came in it since they didn't come around that night. Early the next morning the leader walked into the little church building where Henry was staying, and simply commanded with all authority that we were to go to Boa Vista where Jim and Walnie were. Henry wanted to see his written order, but he simply presented his lieutenant identification card and said he had orders from his General in Manaus - which has to do with *fronteiras*, borders.

After a translated explanation to the people of why we were leaving, we quickly packed and left. He gave us no reason why we were being taken. They followed us in their high powered boat, the lady missionaries in their boat and we in ours. The lieutenant let us sleep in our houses that night, the 27th, telling us we had to be at Tunui, the next Indian village down river, ready to leave by 9:00 a.m. They left for Tunui that afternoon.

At Seringa Ropita, Henry discovered they had broken into his house and had gone through it completely. We were at Tunui and ready to leave at the appointed time. We traveled, from Tunui to here without stopping, except at Tatu. The soldiers were following behind us as the day before, so we just continued until we reached Boa Vista, as he told us. No doubt they slept at the religious leader's place and just got here about an hour ago; the officer was furious! The few Indians here were scared and some wanted to hide in our house, but we made them cooperate with the man's request. All the soldiers came up with bags containing guns.

119

He was angry to find the other missionaries were not here, but had left for the Cubate River. Then he told us that all of us had to be ready to go up to the army post at Cucui, as we were "prisoners". He said Jim and family and Walnie would be taken prisoners too. Then he asked Henry where Sophie was, "She's at the border isn't she?" Henry said he didn't know where she was. "She's going to be taken prisoner too." he said. He demanded to see our passports and visas, which he took. It may be good to notify our American and Canadian Consulates immediately. Elizabeth Koop had left her passport in Manaus so couldn't produce it. Our names are as follows: Myrtle Violet Rehn, Edna F. Loewen, Henry Roland Loewen, Henry James Loewen. The others aren't here so we can't give you their full names and we must get this letter out secretly before the soldiers return - we still don't know why we're being taken, but we are quite sure it's because of the religious leaders.

We're going to Cucui in Henry's launch, tomorrow. Notify our consulates immediately--we need their help also. You there, are our only source of physical help. We don't know how this letter will get out. We continue on in the Hands of our Heavenly Father.

Myrtle

P.S. The officer told the Indians at the village they were to be thrown into the fire if they believed us.

CHAPTER TWENTY-FOUR

ARMY BASE

The Nyengatu Indians stayed with us all day just to show their concern. They had suffered persecution themselves and knew what it felt like and had learned to put their complete trust in the Lord Jesus.

While we waited for the lieutenant to return from arresting the Curtises, the Indian believers reminisced about the times when Sophie Muller was hunted and chased by fanatic authorities. They recalled that at one time when Sophie was teaching in Turtle Village a deputy policeman arrived at the village to take her to Uaupes, the county seat, to face authorities. His helpers were so embarrassed with his drunken condition, they kept him from seeing the American missionary lady and advised the Indians to take her away quickly.

They also remembered when the SPI agent came to get Sophie to take her to Uaupes to face the State prosecutor. When they heard about his coming they whisked her away in a small dugout canoe, paddling upstream as fast as they could. Whenever the agent would be near to catching up with them they'd send her into the woods, sink the canoe near the bank and hide with her while he passed by in his motor boat. They did this several times before the agent gave up and she returned to the village to continue teaching the Nyengatu people again.

The Nyengatus remembered that it was the religious leader who had instigated the authorities to capture her. They believed the same thing was happening now and accepted it as normal for those who followed Jesus Christ. After all didn't Jesus say, "If the world hate you, you know that it hated me before you .... If they have persecuted me they will also persecute you." John 15:18 and 20.

It was just after midday when the soldiers arrived from the Cubate River. All except the officer, greeted me courteously as they pulled alongside our launch. They disembarked and immediately walked up the bank into our motor house and took four cans of our gasoline for their trip back to the army base. Soon I heard the lieutenant yell at the curious Indians. Later on they told me that he had screamed at them while he was telling them it was all just *porcaria* or rubbish the American missionaries taught them. He threatened to punish them if they wouldn't give up their "crazy" ideas.

Antonio told me later on that when he was talking to the officer in Portuguese he had told him he must certainly belong to the religious mission because he spoke Portuguese quite well. Of course, he denied this. The lieutenant had asked him, "Why do you let the foreigners deceive you?"

"The religious leaders are foreigners too," Antonio rebutted.

Merces, who lived farther up river, was there and asked the officer if he was going to pay him for the rock he picked up at his house on his way up river. "No. That rock has no value at all. The Negro River is full of Americans going up every creek looking for gold and other minerals. Why don't you Indians go and look for minerals too?" When the lieutenant had gone up the Isana River, he stopped at many different villages to talk to the people. At Merces' village he had seen a small rock acting as a doorstop. He had accused the Christian Indian of collecting rocks to give to the American missionaries to be sent to the United States. He took the rock with him and left it with the religious leaders for analysis and was told it had no value at all.

In no uncertain terms, he ordered us to get ready to go to Cucui as soon as Jim and Walnie would arrive the next day. Cucui was the Brazilian army base where Colombia and Venezuela join the Brazilian border.

"Who all are supposed to go to Cucui?" was my question.

"You, Jim and Walnie are supposed to go."

Thereupon, they left for Vila Isana for the night and to return their guide who lived there. A few hours later the other missionaries arrived from their aborted teaching trip on the Cubate River. Jim and Skip, his wife, wondered what was going on and wasted no time asking us what was happening.

Some days before all this happened while the Curtises and Walnie Kliewer were getting ready to spend a few weeks on the Cubate River they were interrupted in their preparations by the arrival of seven men in a boat. They had chatted with them and asked where they came from and where they were going. The men had told them that they were from Manaus and were going up to Tunui to look for rubber and wood. After they left the missionaries thought it was quite strange, because everybody knew there was little or no rubber in the area. However, they soon forgot about the strangers as they prepared to leave.

That weekend they were teaching Bible in the village with plans to start literacy classes the first day of the week. Some were already arriving from other villages for the classes to begin when they heard an outboard motor in the distance. It turned out to be the same boat and the same men that had stopped at the mission station a few days before.

Jim asked the leader if they had found the rubber and wood they were looking for. Without responding, he produced his military identification card and said he was the commanding officer of the army base at Cucui. And, as such, he ordered them to pack up and get ready immediately to go to Cucui.

"I have already arrested the other missionaries from upriver and Sophie Muller will be captured on the Colombian border." When the missionaries asked him to show his order to arrest them he replied, "I don't need any written order, I am in command." When the missionaries expressed doubts about obeying his orders he told them unequivocally that if they would not go on their own they would take them by force. He said the men with him were armed soldiers.

"Why are you taking us away?" Jim asked.

"Because of the fight between the believers and the religious leaders."

"What fight?"

"You'll find out later on," had been his scathing reply.

"We will go on ahead to Cucui and you are to follow just as soon as possible," was his final command to them. Within the hour the Curtises and Walnie were on their way and arrived, just before sunset, at their station, where we were waiting for them.

Now we didn't feel so alone any more with our co-workers present. I kept on remembering the message Antonio gave on Sunday morning saying we are to rejoice when they speak all sorts of evil against us and persecute us. God brought to my attention Luke 6:23 where it says we are to rejoice and leap for joy when we are reproached for Christ's sake. Well, I certainly didn't feel like rejoicing, much less like jumping for joy. I didn't like this whole thing. The Indian believers depended on our teaching. They were new in the faith and needed someone to instruct them in the Christian faith and walk.

"Lord, forgive my unbelief," I prayed, "and teach me to be thankful in this situation even though I do not know what is going on. Give me your joy now as I am being reproached because of the Name of Christ." God met my need and filled my heart with a deep satisfaction and joy as I gave in to Him. I began to understand what Luke meant when he said "leap for joy".

Early in the morning, while getting the last things ready to go, we heard a high-speed outboard motor passing the mouth of the river heading up the Negro River. We believed the lieutenant and his men had stayed overnight at Vila Isana. Not too much later we stopped at the first village to take Francisco along to be our guide on the way to Cucui. We discovered him standing at the river's edge while his wife and mother stood farther up the bank crying. He told us immediately that the lieutenant and his soldiers had just been there and had been extremely rude to him.

The lieutenant had told him, "If you're an American and think yourself better than everybody else, don't you know that they are all going to be ordered off the Negro river?" He also asked, "Are you a believer?"

"Yes," Francisco answered courageously. "I'm a believer in Jesus Christ."

"Then that's the reason you are going all over the Isana River mistreating everyone!" The lieutenant had accused him of various things, tied him up with cords at the point of a loaded gun and warned him to stay in his village and keep quiet about his religion. Then he added, "If there are any more reports about you going around teaching, I will come and beat you up and take you prisoner too." Then he had continued his trip. Francisco couldn't come with us because his brother-in-law had been bitten by a snake and he needed to stay with him.

The lieutenant was eating lunch when we arrived at the army base in Cucui and didn't want to be disturbed. When he had finished he told us that by mid-afternoon he would receive word from the Army General in Manaus telling him what to do with us. We were at liberty to move about as we wished. We talked to some of the soldiers who were off duty and shared the Gospel with them. In the morning we were called in and the officer took Jim's and Walnie's passports and other documents from them. We asked him to tell us the reason for taking us away from our ministry.

"I'll be glad to tell you," the lieutenant replied contemptuously. "You are teaching the believers to attack the religious leaders. You order poisoning among the believers. You cause misery among the believers. You instigated the burning of a religious mission chapel and you order them to destroy their images. You teach the believers not to plant because of Christ's soon return. You prohibit the raising of pigs and chickens. You Americanize the Indians and order them to destroy anything they buy at the religious mission . You tell the believers to persecute those belonging to the religious missions." Then he told us that we are not in the dark ages any longer and there is religious freedom in Brazil!

Back again in our boat we wrote down all the accusations while they were still fresh in our minds. At about three in the afternoon we were interrupted by two soldiers who brought us three cans of gasoline to repay the four the lieutenant had taken at Boa Vista. The gasoline was so dirty we didn't take it. Later he paid for it in cash.

A short while later Lieutenant Licciardi called for us and told us he had received orders from Manaus we were to go there on the FAB (Brazilian Air Force) plane the 10th of February. He ordered us to get our families from Boa Vista and be back in Cucui on the 9th.

It was late in the afternoon when we left the army base. Our guide suggested we stop before it got dark because he was not well acquainted with the channel with the dangerous rocks in that part of the river. At break of dawn we were on the way again and arrived at Francisco's village just in time for his brother-in-law's burial. Everyone was very sad, so we spent some time with them to encourage them in the Word.

It was a short distance to the mission station, so we arrived by late afternoon. The women wanted to hear what had happened to us while we were in Cucui. We told them about everything before we began to get things ready to go back to the army base and on to Manaus. There was bimonthly plane service at Vila Isana, the nearest settlement on the Negro River.

We decided to ask David Sharp to return to Manaus on the next commercial plane to take our urgent letters to our mission leader. David had finished high school in the mission's school and was visiting the Curtis family. We also asked Francisco to accompany David to testify on our behalf, if needed.

We had a good visit with the two elderly brothers who own the settlement at Vila Isana. Neither one of them had known anything about our arrest by the lieutenant. But Jorge, who had been hired by the lieutenant to be his guide on the Isana River, said he felt very uneasy and many times had been embarrassed by the lieutenant's behavior. They were all very sympathetic to us and showed real concern. Through the years these folks had been very kind to us evangelical missionaries although when the Gospel first entered the area the oldest brother was very hostile to the missionaries.

A few days later, the second lieutenant from Cucui arrived in a speed boat early in the morning to inform us that the Brazilian Air Force plane would arrive two days earlier than we had been told. We were to leave for Cucui right away! We explained to the officer that under no circumstances could we arrive there within such a short time in our launch.

As an alternative, he told us to go to Vila Isana and wait there for the FAB plane to pick us up. However, in case it did not arrive there, then we were to go to Cucui as previously planned.

The lieutenant and his two privates had breakfast with Jim and Skip, after which they had a good look at Jim's radio antenna.

"What kind of a radio do you have?" he asked Jim.

"That is a simple antenna for my radio receiver," he responded.

"Do you have a transceiver radio?" he confronted him.

"No sir, I do not have a transceiver radio."

"How then do you communicate with your people in Manaus?" was his next question.

"We send mail down to Manaus whichever way we can," Jim answered with finality.

The FAB plane did not land at Vila Isana, which meant we'd have to take the launch all the way upriver to Cucui.

CHAPTER TWENTY-FIVE

WE'RE QUESTIONED

Progress against the current was slow due to the long detours we had to make around shallow areas where sand bars appeared above the black water. Huge boulders just beneath the surface of the water were a constant threat. There were ten of us crowded into the boat: Jim and Skip Curtis with their small son George, Elizabeth Koop, Myrtle Rehn, Walnie Kliewer, Edna, our son Jim, myself and Antonio our guide, going to the army base at Cucui as ordered by Lieutenant Licciardi.

It was early in the morning a few days later when we arrived in Cucui. We reported to the lieutenant right away. He told us we were all to sleep in our launch and have our meals there.

"Sir, the launch is too small to accommodate all of us for any length of time. We feel that since you commanded us to come here, you are responsible for our lodging and meals," I boldly told him. He did not expect this from me, since I had been quite submissive so far. He thought for a bit.

"Okay, you men will stay in one building and the women and children will stay in another," he retorted. "You will have your meals in my quarters," he added.

The ladies and children were lodged in one empty classroom and the men in another. We were free to wander around the army base. After a few meals with him, the lieutenant appeared to be very uneasy about having us in his quarters for our meals. We asked him if we could have our meals with the soldiers in the mess hall.

The next day our friend Senhor Athayde Cardoso arrived. He was the local agent of the Service for the Protection of the Indians - SPI . It seemed like the lieutenant had asked him to be there at this time. The officer took a long time telling him all the things we were accused of doing among the Indians. Later on Sr. Athayde told us he was quite shocked at all this and said he told the lieutenant the very opposite was true. He encouraged us and said he was going to go up into the Isana River to check into all the allegations. He told us with certainty that all these accusations originated with the religious leaders.

For the next few days we were free to move about among the soldiers who were not on duty. The ladies taught the cook how to make some simple desserts for the soldiers. They all loved the "globs" they made with rolled oats and chocolate. This opened the door wide open to talk to all of them.

The Air Force plane finally arrived on Thursday bringing Major Severiano Hermes and some lieutenants. We were to get ready to leave the next morning. We took our launch to a sheltered spot in a nearby creek indicated by one of the local merchants who also owned a boat. Before we could secure the boat and leave it in charge of a local man, we got a message from Lieutenant Licciardi to present ourselves to him right away. We wondered if he was afraid we were trying to escape.

It was almost five o'clock when we were told that Major Severiano Hermes wanted to interrogate each one of us separately right after supper.

The interrogation team consisted of Major Severiano Hermes, Lieutenant Licciardi and another lieutenant who was a military clerk. I was instructed that after they would be done with questioning me I was not to talk to the other missionaries.

Q. "How many years have you been on the Isana River?"

A. "Since 1954."

Q. "Do you teach the Indians Portuguese?"

A. "Yes, at times."

Q. "Why not always?"

A. "Religious instruction is given in Baniwa."

Q. "Why do you teach the Indians not to eat salt?"

A. 'We do not teach them not to eat salt."

Q. "Why do you teach the Indians not to buy at the religious mission?"

A. "We advise them to buy with any merchant that comes along." Then I added that a certain religious leader had forbidden them (the believers) to appear at his mission.

Q. "Why do you instruct the Indians to attack the religious leaders?"

A. "We do not. We teach them to be kind to all. The fact is that the religious leader insults the Indians when he gets to their villages. He calls them all kinds of names such as, pig, dog, billy goat and the like."

Q. "Why do you teach the Indians to marry at 12 or 13 years of age?"

A. "We do not."

Q. "Why do you destroy chapels and images of the religious mission?"

A. "We do not."

Then Lieutenant Licciardi said that this happened in Valentim's village (Frog Point). I told him the religious mission chapel was still standing in that village at the time we passed there when he arrested us and the image had been taken away some time ago.

Q. "What do you know about five Indians being poisoned in May 1960 and seven in June 1960?"

A. "Nothing."

Q. "Why do you teach the Indians to poison those who do not want to become Protestants?"

A. "We do not."

Q. "Are you aware of the fact that they poison each other in the *cuias* - gourds?"

A. "I know nothing about this."

Then I explained that whenever an Indian is sick, he first thinks of poison. We have treated many with worm treatment and vitamins when they thought they were poisoned. We did not think they were poisoned but were sick of natural causes.

Q. "What is *maraka imbara*?"

A. "This, as far as I know, is poison."

Q. "What does *matiara* mean?"

A. "Demons or evil spirits, as far as I know."

Q. "Why do you teach the Indians they are Americans?"

A. "We do not. On the contrary we teach them they are Brazilians and they have reason to be proud of it."

Q. "Where does your money come from?"

A. "Our church in Canada. They send it to NTM in America from where it is sent to Sao Paulo where it is exchanged into Brazilian currency and then sent to us in Manaus."

Q. "How much do you get?"

A. "We each get $75 per month."

Q. "How did you buy your fridge and duplicator and etc.?"

A. "We bought these little by little as we had money."

Q. "What do you know about Sophie Muller?"

A. "I know she is teaching Indians in Colombia."

Q. "Does she order you missionaries around in Brazil?"

A. "No."

Q. "Is she your 'head'?"

A. "No."

Q. "Who is?"

A. "Mr. Macon Hare."

Q. "Where is he?"

A. "In Manaus."

Q. "Is he American?"

A. "Yes."

Q. "Do you ever see Sophie Muller?"

A. "Yes."

Q. "Why?"

A. "We pay her cordial visits coinciding with our travels near the border."

Q. "What do you know about shipping minerals to the United States?"

A. "Nothing."

Q. "Have you climbed the mountain near Tunui?"

A. "No."

Q. "Have you planned a trip up there?"

A. "No. A couple of years ago a mineralogist from Manaus went up the Tunui mountain. He had come in Sr. Athayde's launch on one of his regular trips. Whether or not the two were connected I do not know."

Q. "Does Sr. Athayde have a real good boat?"

A. "No, I guess nothing special. In fact on one occasion he borrowed nails from me to make repairs on it."

Q. "When did he last pass Tunui?"

A. "I don't know."

Q. "Within the year 1960?"

A. "I don't think so."

Q. "Does Sr. Athayde trade precious stones with the Indians."

A. "I don't know."

Q. "Does Sr. Athayde belong to the religious mission?"

A. "Yes, he says so himself."

Q. "Does he have any troubles with the religious leaders?"

A. "I do not know about his personal life."

When the questioning was over, I was asked to sign my statement. Major Hermes and the clerk also signed it.

After this I was reminded not to talk with the others until after they had been interrogated, and an armed guard would be watching me. All the other missionaries were questioned, one by one, which lasted until about 2:00 a.m.

CHAPTER TWENTY-SIX

CUCUI, INTERROGATIONS

As we were about to board the Brazilian Air Force plane, the officer demanded, "What is in that bottle?" when he saw a small glass bottle containing greyish powder in Jim Curtis's bag. The expression on the officer's face seemed to say, Here is the evidence that the missionaries are actually searching for minerals after all! Here is the proof and I catch them red-handed!

"Oh, that is just plain gold dust," Jim replied mockingly.

"Open it up," the officer commanded.

"Why? Do you want to try some? It is only powdered pepper I got from the Indians."

The bag was closed, loaded into the plane and we were off.

The Canadian-built Catalina plane barely reached flying altitude when it landed at a religious mission station and took on a number of baskets of manioc flour. At Tapuruquara the plane took on fuel, and the manioc flour was taken off for the religious mission there. The pilots and officers were brought hot meals from the religious mission . We were given the leftovers!

Major Zobaran met us in Manaus around two in the afternoon and ordered us to remain within the limits of the city and to appear at the Army General's headquarters at eight the next morning.

We arrived at the Army Headquarters on time only to be ignored for two hours when we were told to return again at four in the afternoon. Little did we realize how frustrated the high ranking army officers were at our arrest. They did not know what to do with us. They did not want to admit their error nor did they want to proceed with this unjustified arrest. It was unlawful for the armed forces to be involved in any religious questions.

We were back again on time. Elizabeth and Myrtle were taken in together. Then Edna and I were interrogated together. Later on I made a list of the questions they asked.

Q. "What do you teach the Indians?"

A. "The Bible, Baniwa and Portuguese languages and some arithmetic."

A. "How many hours of their time do you take daily?"

A. "Usually an hour in the evening unless they are free otherwise."

Q. "Do you have ten-day, or longer, reunions with them?"

A. "No."

Q. "Do you have a permit from the SPI.

A. "Yes."

Q. "Where is it?"

A. "In the house."

They asked me to bring it to them the following day, Sunday, at ten in the morning.

Q. "Do you know what this is?"

A. "Yes, it is a map. I made it."

Q. "Why did you make it?"

A. "For my own use to know where the villages are located on the Isana River."

Q. "Why did you give it to the SPI agent?"

A. "I showed it to Sr. Tubal, he liked it and I gave it to him."

Q. "How many did you make?"

A. "Two."

Q. "On what scale?"

A. "It is a copy of the Aeronautical Chart."

Then they asked me to sit down at a table while they repeated all the questions and wrote them down together with my answers. However, the army auditor went into much more detail in questioning me about my personal life; furlough, Betty's death, my remarriage and return to Brazil, and so on. Then I signed the statement and we were free to go. Edna wasn't questioned at all. Jim and Walnie were questioned separately.

That day did not really feel as if it were Sunday. We had committed ourselves to God completely. We did not know what would happen but we did know that we had His promise to be with us regardless of circumstances.

Our legal permits to work with the Indians were seized at the army headquarters. The Colonel told us they were invalid. What we didn't know at that time was that the General had sent a radiogram to the head of the SPI, requesting him to annul our permits.

One of the majors told me the Indians were not like other people. They did not have souls like the rest of us. "They are like horses and other animals, without souls. You are wasting your time working with them."

Our mission director was interrogated the same morning. We were told that our permits would be returned to us again. Edna was thoroughly grilled with an official interpreter, since she did not as yet have a good command of Portuguese

This took several hours. Then we were told we were free to go and if anything new should turn up we should feel free to return and talk things over with them. We could bring our lawyers or consuls.

Early the following morning a soldier appeared at the door and left a note saying that one of the men from the Isana work should appear at the army headquarters at two-thirty that afternoon. Jim and I went to see what they wanted now. All they wanted was to return our passports and documents. We asked if we were free to visit our school children at Puraquequara. The major replied that within 24 hours he would have an answer for us. Several days later no answer had come so we appealed to the British Consul who received a two day leave for us to visit our children at the boarding school down river from Manaus.

We hadn't seen our children, who were at boarding school, since the lieutenant captured us and we were taken away from our work. They were full of questions and eager to hear what had happened to us. They told us they had prayed very much for us ever since they heard we had been arrested and it had been very hard for them. Being children, they soon ran off to join their friends.

CHAPTER TWENTY-SEVEN

INTERROGATIONS AND WAITING

The military authorities were quite puzzled as to how we sent word of our capture to Manaus while we were still on the Isana River. At various times we were asked about our radio transmitter which, of course, we did not possess. The only possible way we had was with a passenger, or a package, on Panair's bi-monthly plane service.

Apparently David Sharp's name was not included on the list of missionaries, so the lieutenant ignored him and never referred to him. It worked out very well to have him return to Manaus, sooner than planned, on Panair's bi-monthly service. He had an important part to play in this whole fiasco.

"All missionaries on Isana held prisoner by Brazilian Army. Arrive in Manaus 10th for questioning. Pray," read the telegram Bob Rich, our buyer and shipper, immediately sent to Mission headquarters in the USA. Macon Hare, our field chairman, wasted no time getting word out to the British consul.

Interestingly enough, the consul habitually joined the local Army General for a nightly drink in the luxurious Hotel Amazonas. That evening he questioned the General about the missionaries being arrested by an army lieutenant. The General was aware of the missionaries' arrest, but was taken by complete surprise at the consul's question. How could he be informed so quickly? Surely the missionaries must have a two-way radio. He felt very uncomfortable. This could turn into an international incident.

Several days later Macon Hare, our field director, sent a telegram to mission headquarters in the US: "Missionaries due tomorrow. General will not permit lawyer in trial. Accusation homicide. See letter."

Before we ever arrived at the army base in Cucui, the Canadian and American Departments of External Affairs were notified of our arrest. They were concerned that our children be well taken care of during this time and took measures to insure this. Our church in Canada was informed as well and they prayed. The whole time, we were unaware of what was going on. We only knew we were being held against our wishes and could do nothing but cooperate with the lieutenant's orders.

At the same time, in Canada, the head of the State Department reported "he had received another telegram from our Embassy in Rio de Janeiro, reporting that after a military hearing in Manaus, which neither the missionaries' lawyer nor any consular representative were permitted to attend, the charges had been dropped and all the missionaries were freed. The missionaries had been informed that they had been living in a security area without proper legal permission. Although this was the first intimation they had this was so, it appears the real reason for the arrest may have been the Brazilian Army's desire to remove the foreigners from the area."

Our case was turned over to the Brazilian National Security Council and was, therefore, not an open case. Everything was done without our knowledge.

Donald Reimer, Secretary Treasurer of Reimer Express Lines, a good friend of Edna's family, inquired of the Secretary of State for External Affairs Canada for information about the state of our detention. He received the following telegram: "I am asking officials of my department to let you know immediately when they have any further news about Henry and Edna Loewen. In the meantime, you may assure Mrs. Loewen's mother that everything possible is being done to safeguard the interests of the Loewen family."

From our point of view the story was quite different. True, we were not permitted to have a lawyer nor a consular representative with us during the hearings. Everything appeared to be very secretive. At one point I made mention, in the lieutenant's presence, that he had told us very plainly that we were prisoners. This the lieutenant denied very forcefully. When all the questioning was finished, we were led to believe we were arrested because we were not properly documented and were in the frontier zone illegally. No further mention was made of the alleged involvement of the religious mission. We were also told that the Brazilian army could not interfere in religious affairs. Major Severiano Hermes told me he was a direct descendant of the Brazilian Army Marshall who was a leader in promoting freedom of religion in Brazil and the expulsion of the Jesuits because of their constant interference in governmental affairs.

Brazilian friends began sending us letters deploring the fact that we had been detained by the Army. Joao Evangelista Lima wrote to Whom it May Concern:

In the capacity of former secretary in the office of the Municipality of Uaupes, in the State of Amazonas, located on the upper Rio Negro, exactly in the "Boundary Zone" to which Law n° 2,597, of September 12, 1955, makes reference, and being fully acquainted with everything of that region I consider myself qualified to declare that the religious policy accepted and put in practice by the religious mission, against New Tribes Evangelical Mission, a mission led, in a superior manner, by American evangelists, is nothing but a repugnant smear campaign involving the indigenous people.

I am not catholic, atheist nor protestant. I have no intention of protecting anyone in this case under consideration, neither do I wish that this affirmation contain favoritism or partiality What I am saying is because of justice, of law and truth; for I do not have the slightest doubt that which motivates the religious leaders against the American evangelists is simply a crusade of aggression, defamation, and lies, carried on by the envy and resentment by those who see the progress and success obtained by the Americans, both in the field of religious teaching and the cultural advancement of the people of the region.

It is publicly well known in Uaupes that, by their constant toil, by their methods of rapid teaching, by the almost miraculous operation of the Americans, the life of the indigenous people of the Isana River, where the so-called "Evangelical Mission" is stationed, went through such a transformation it is difficult to believe without seeing and without a reliable investigation, the former life of the Indians in contrast to the pattern of their present life and their conduct towards their own. Buying on credit and cheating the merchant; lying; practicing the demonic *juruparis* which almost always leads to crime; doing *caxiris*, drinking without restraint, dancing; smoking and extravagant drinking, was, formerly the greatest enjoyment of the Indians of the Isana River. Today, however, none of this happens. Those who have entered into the "American Evangelical Mission" do not practice any of this. They do not buy on credit. When they buy, they do not cheat. They don't lie, they don't smoke, nor drink and dance. And, which is even more commendable, they abandoned all the traditional indigenous customs, and they know how to read and write!!! Those *Isaneiros* , dwellers on the Isana, who received teaching from the Americans, have acquired a true concept of responsibility. Today they are civilized men, honest, respectable and worthy of trust. But, not only this, if this energy and labor of the American evangelicals deserves our acclaim and admiration, it is no less admirable to know they accomplished all this in a record time of three to four years without one cent of liability to the treasury of the Nation.

As for the Italian, religious leaders who overrun almost all of the Rio Negro and its tributaries, what have they done during the 46 years in contrast to that done by the American Protestants? Nothing. Nothing besides building scores and scores of comfortable buildings, to their own advantage, and yearly spending 200 million of the people's cruzeiros, in exchange for a sad and poorly administered literacy program. From this point they began to slander and to lie. Their design being the expulsion of the American benefactors, the enslavement of the people, whom they strive to maintain in ignorance, and the total dominion of the region.

The accusations which they formulated and recently sent to the National Army, having in mind, like we already said, the eviction of the Americans from the upper Isana River. This gives us proven evidence of the defamatory battle they wage against the Americans, since they accumulate into a dung heap of lies and decay. But, the Brazilian Army, maintaining its tradition of honor and dignity, certainly will not be carried away by insubstantial insinuations nor will it take biased or precipitated procedures against the Protestants, without the opening of an accurate inquiry in the place of the accusations and without a complete investigation around them in order to obtain the necessary clarification of the truth.

The high ranking officers of the Army know the law previously referred to, which monitors the "Boundary Zones" is incomplete with regards to religious worship, and the Americans under discussion, did not incur any infraction foreseen in the above mentioned Law. If this happens, that is, if there is someone within that region who acts contrary to these legal regulations in the "Boundary Zone", this someone would be the "religious mission" which take hold of large areas, opening up roads and smuggling entirely without the knowledge of the Brazilian authorities. If, in face of all this, the permanence of the Italian religious leaders are tolerated in the "Boundary Zone", then this measure or this tolerance should be extended to the American Protestants, since all foreigners are on an equal bases.

This document which encompasses the naked and raw truth without any constraint, may be used for legal purposes, under any circumstance or eventuality, for it conveys the truth, I repeat, and for which I assume all responsibility.

MANAUS, April 03, 1961
Signed: Joao Evangelista Lima

Duly signed registered by:
ROSALVO BRAGA GUALBERTO,
Notary Public in Manaus the 3rd day of April 1961.

Luiz Monteiro da Cruz, a well educated son of Portuguese immigrants to Brazil, became an accountant in a sugar factory. As a young man, he had become a Christian. He married and raised a family. After early retirement he took some Bible courses and consequently became part of New Tribes Mission of Brazil.

Senhor Luiz, as we called him affectionately, was a very good leader and dedicated believer. When the mission was in need of a president he was the best choice, not only because he was Brazilian, but because of his mature Christian character. He was extremely troubled when he heard we had been arrested in the State of Amazonas. He immediately conferred with his brother, Armando, who was a Federal Representative in Brasilia, a medical doctor as well as a major in the army. Sr. Armando was outraged and promised to look into this immediately. He conferred with other evangelical Federal Representatives in order to get their opinion on this serious matter.

He began by calling a congressional hearing of the Service for the Protection of the Indian - SPI. The director of the SPI was called to give a detailed report of all the activities of the service and many irregularities were uncovered. Some time later Colonel Moacyr Ribeiro Coelho, the newly appointed director of the SPI, discovered some flagrant illegalities when he questioned us about the activities of some of the agents who were thereupon dismissed from the service.

By this time we had taken on a different assignment while we waited for our clearance to return to our work. We assumed the responsibility of dorm parents for about twenty boarding school children in grades one to four. This certainly was different from tribal work, but we enjoyed it. In our daily evening devotions with all the children we prayed for God to work in the hearts of the Brazilian authorities, and especially for the salvation of the new director of the Service for the Protection of the Indians.

The new director of the SPI appointed by the Federal government was a very patriotic officer of the Brazilian Army. It appeared to us he might have been appointed director of the SPI to get rid of all foreign missionaries working with Indians, especially along the international border. However, when he inspected the work among the Pacaas Novos tribe, he discovered that the money the Brazilian government had allotted to help these Indians had been used in other ways to benefit the religious mission; whereas, the evangelical missionaries had spent their own personal income to buy medication for sick Indians. He was infuriated by this and determined to give the evangelical missionaries back their permits to work with the indigenous people.

Sr. Luiz arranged a meeting with the new SPI director and asked me to accompany him. We met in Brasilia and spend time together in prayer asking God to work in the heart of this new director. There was quite a bit of walking to be done to reach the ministry in which the SPI had its offices; and by the time we got there Sr. Luiz's feet hurt so badly he could barely walk. He breathed a sigh of relief when we got there and could rest before seeing the colonel.

It was a long time before he called us in and when he finally did he seemed to be under much pressure. We discussed the work of the mission among the various tribes in Brazil. He kept asking questions and soon it was time to leave, but he asked us to stay a little longer. When we saw his secretary was leaving, we got up to leave too but he insisted we stay even though the office closed. He told us about the extreme pressure that was on him from the religious mission because they perceived he favored us over them. He didn't know how long he could take the pressure. In his wisdom, Sr. Luiz encouraged him to trust God to give him wisdom in his difficult job and asked for permission to pray with him. Before going he asked the colonel if he would accept a copy of the Bible. "Yes, I would like that very much," he replied in a tired voice.

As soon as we left the Ministry of Agriculture building, Sr. Luiz said he felt like jumping for joy and said his feet didn't feel as though he were walking on ground. The next day we delivered a Bible to the colonel with his name engraved on the cover.

The Army General in command in the Amazonas area during our arrest also appeared before the congressional hearing. One of the first questions he was asked was about his ongoing dispute with Colonel Moacyr Ribeiro Coelho, the newly appointed director of the SPI. He denied ever having had any controversy with the Colonel. Although, later on, he admitted that his disagreement with the Colonel was because of his desire to reinstate the missionaries in the tribe. The fact was when the Colonel talked to me about reissuing our permits he mentioned, out of respect, he first needed to see the General. And, he added, he and the General had always been at odds with each other.

The General testified he had received a request for help from the religious mission because they were being attacked and their chapels burned by Indians led by protestant missionaries. He received the first accusations and soon the second without taking any action. But when the accusations were repeated the third time, he decided to send the commander of the Army Base in Cucui to check into the matter.

He testified that the young, impetuous officer, believing the accusations were true, captured the missionaries and took them to the Army Base in Cucui. Thereupon, the American consul, on request of the Pentagon and the American Congress, approached him for information about the apprehension. The General then told the U.S. government officials they could see by this what enormous resources the missionaries had out there on the frontier. He said they had everything: airplanes, launches, medicines as much as they wanted, and they frequently received money from the American Senate.

How ironic! The General believed we had greater access to medical supplies for the Indians than the SPI, which was an agency of the federal government. He did not know how often we had begged for medicines to treat the Indians and how often we had been turned down. God made the small amounts of medicine we were able to purchase with our allowance, go much farther than we ever expected.

The General informed the congressional hearing that an army officer wanted to release the missionaries but he himself had ordered an investigation to be held by another superior officer, Major Severiano Hermes.

Churches in Manaus were very sympathetic but were afraid to openly help us because of the military pressure. Even our lawyer, a fine Christian man and pastor of a local church, was very hesitant because of the power of the army in Brazil. But he prayed with us and carefully took note of all the events we reported to him.

A local politician told us he had had a conversation with a man in charge of placing army officials in various places across the country. He was told a religious mission dignitary had asked him to suggest the transfer of a General to Manaus who was devoted to the religious mission and a devout officer, to Cucui. More and more we realized the power of those who opposed the Gospel of the Lord Jesus Christ.

Things were moving in Brasilia, the nation's new capital. The National Security Council took up our case, not because we requested it but because of its nature. The decision of these men would be final. God had His men in high places too. The National Security Council, which consisted of magistrates and high ranking military officers, debated our case after reading what had been written by military officials and the congressional investigation. They had copies of the accusations against us and of our own depositions.

Sr. Luiz's brother had been a member of this Council some years ago and now had a good friend presiding over it. He kept him informed of the progress they were making. Then one day he told him that we missionaries were free to return to our work and within a month we should have full clearance from the military in Manaus, but no notice came.

We waited. No word from the army headquarters in Manaus. What should we do now? Our lawyer agreed with Major Hermes' suggestion we go to the army headquarters in Belem since the local General was subordinate to the one there. He had a friend in government there who knew a very influential colonel stationed there. He offered to write to his friend asking him to inform the colonel about the case and to tell him that Jim Curtis and I were going there to see him.

After a two hour flight we were in Belem, at the mouth of the Amazon River. We booked into a hotel and made our way to the army headquarters. There one of the guards took us into the main building to see the colonel who addressed us in perfect English. He had taken military courses in the USA. He informed us the General was meeting with all his officers in a few minutes and nobody was available to see us.

"Can you return this afternoon?" he asked us.

"We certainly can, sir," was our reply.

He ordered one of the privates to take us to our hotel and pick us up for the two o'clock interview. Turning to us again he said: "There will be four majors, to listen to your case." Then he pointed out the four majors who were standing nearby.

Promptly at two we were ushered into a fair-sized room where we met with the four officers. After introductions we told them Major Severiano Hermes had advised us to plead our case here. We told them our mission had been on the Isana River since 1952, evangelizing and teaching the Indians to read and write in their own language as well as the Portuguese language and some rudiments of arithmetic.

They took note that we did not own property in the tribal area and the place we were located was authorized by the agent of the SPI. They also made a note, in their report, that we did not own any prospecting equipment; we did not own transceiver radios but had radios only to get the news, and other programs, we used only the Panair plane service to take our mail. They further made mention, in their report, that if we violated any laws of the country we agreed it would be right for us to be removed from the area where we worked. The report mentioned we would, very much, like to be visited by Military officers in order for them to see firsthand, the work we were doing among the Indians. The majors also stated, in the report that we showed them our newly issued, valid permits to work with Indians, signed by Colonel Moacyr Ribeiro Coelho, director of the SPI.

Later the General read the report, discussed it with the four majors and came to the conclusion that we were free to return to our work among the Indians on the Isana River. We were told to return to Manaus and wait for word from the local army headquarters and if within five days we weren't notified, we were to send them a telegram in Belem.

A few days later, back in Manaus, a soldier appeared early in the morning with a written notice that we were to appear at the army headquarters. We were excited about this. Yet we wondered what they would say. A Brazilian Air Force lieutenant had already warned us more complaints were being filed against us by the religious leaders from the Isana River area. He said they were accusing us of ordering the Christian Indians to burn others who didn't want to believe like they did.

Jim Curtis and I presented ourselves to a Colonel Alipio who told us he had received orders from the General in Belem and we were free to return to our work on the Isana.

"But," he added quickly, "you are not going to go."

"Why not?" Jim and I asked, almost in unison.

"I'll tell you," he replied, with an air of haughty superiority.

CHAPTER TWENTY-EIGHT

CONFUSION BEFORE RETURN

"There are new accusations against you," the Colonel Alipio said cynically.

"Are you at liberty to tell us what these charges are?" we asked him.

"Yes, most certainly."

"The allegations are that you have been sending gasoline to the Christian Indians on the Isana River to burn those of their own people who do not want to adopt your religion".

"That is absurd. We haven't sent any gasoline to the Isana River since we were removed from there. This is a serious mistake."

"That is the accusation against you and we will not permit you to return," he said flatly.

"Would you please tell us where these accusations come from?"

"Yes. These accusations came to us from a highly esteemed religious leader."

"In that case, may we return with our lawyer?" we asked.

"You may do that," he replied.

We wasted no time to inform our lawyer of this new turn of events. Our lawyer was very disturbed at this and realized this was not a military matter any more but a religious one. He had also been previously informed, by the same Air Force officer who warned us about these allegations by the religious leader, and had been thinking of a way to handle this.

Colonel Alipio did not really expect us back again so soon. Our lawyer proposed that since there were three parties in this case, then all three parties should be involved in a thorough investigation. He suggested that the army officers, the religious leaders and we missionaries get together, preferably on the Isana River, and look into this matter. The colonel agreed to our lawyer's proposal that all three parties should meet on the Isana River. He said he would let us know when this would take place.

We waited. Weeks went by and then we heard the Air Force plane had gone to the Isana River and had returned. We had not been notified.

Our lawyer advised us to ask Colonel Alipio permission for Jim Curtis and his family to return to their station near the mouth of the Isana River. To our surprise the request was granted. The Curtises began preparations immediately and soon were on their way back after being gone almost two years.

A few months later Edna and I were given the permission to return as well. We began preparations to go. Our launch was in Manaus and we'd return with it. Antonio, my Baniwa informant, who had been with me in Manaus, helping me translate the New Testament into his language, was willing to guide us back along the hundreds of miles of treacherous river.

Then a telegram arrived for Edna telling her that her mother had cancer with about three months to live. This was a shock! Having been out of the tribe for two years and now being free to return we got this urgent telegram. We were cast upon God again. This was very hard for Edna. She loved her mother dearly and would so much love to be with her in her final suffering. She prayed much. We prayed together and waited upon God for direction. I suggested that Edna go to be with her mother while I would return to the Isana River to finish up the remaining few months of translation work.

One morning she told me. "Henry, I promised, on our wedding day, to go wherever you went. Remember we made that promise to each other taken from the book of Ruth? 'Entreat me not to leave thee, or to return from following after thee: for whither thou goest, I will go; and where thou lodgest, I will lodge: thy people shall be my people, and thy God my God.'" Edna also remembered her mother had told her, "Don't ever return to be with me if I get sick. God's work is more important." She made the decision to stay and was satisfied she was doing the right thing.

Before leaving Manaus with our launch, we asked the person in charge of our mail that if we should get a telegram about Edna's mother to give us this message on the commercial radio station giving messages to those living far from the city. We promised to listen every day.

Our hearts rejoiced. We were returning to the people we have known and loved for many years. We had been gone two years.

As we traveled we wondered what changes might have taken place in our absence. Would some have become weak in their faith? Would some have returned to their old ways? We discussed this with Antonio, our guide, as we steadily moved up the Negro River. In all our teaching we had always stressed the point that they should not build on us, the missionaries, but only on the Word of God. We could change or even leave, but the Word of God would always remain the same.

As we got closer, we had to stop at the impassable rapids at the town of Uaupes. The local people were happy to see us and soon they transported all our baggage to a point above the rapids. The boat had to be as light as possible to be able to navigate the swift, turbulent water between those

146

huge boulders. The town's most experienced river pilot was willing to take our boat through the torrent. His breath smelled of liquor but he seemed quite capable of handling the wheel. He was in control and wanted me to stand near the motor for any eventuality, or, maybe to keep me away from the wheel. Antonio was on board too. He enjoyed this kind of excitement. Edna and six-year-old Jimmy watched from the rock on the river bank along with a number of local people. She prayed for our safe passage.

The guide steered the boat into the backwash behind a granite boulder. There we gained speed before he guided the boat straight into the smooth, swift water of the main channel. For a moment it seemed like the launch was stopped. The propeller turned as fast as it could. I wondered if anything would go wrong with the propeller turning faster than it had for some time and then the pilot asked me above the roar of the fifty-two horse power diesel engine: "Can you speed up the motor a bit more?"

There was a slight increase in speed as I forced the throttle. We moved ever so slightly. We were heading toward the other side of the smooth, rushing channel. The guide had told us on a previous occasion that the water is alive and it continually changes so now he had to wait for this change when the propeller could grab the water. Soon we were gaining ever so little. Yes, we were moving forward. We were going to make it!

The guide relaxed, looked at me and said jubilantly, "We made it!" Those on shore cheered for us, happy that our boat had not crashed against the rocks. Once again God had faithfully taken us through dangerous waters. Four more hours of dangerous traveling were ahead of us before we would be through this part of the river, with its countless boulders rising threateningly above the surface, while others lay ominously beneath the surface.

Every place we stopped along the river the people greeted us gladly and asked how we were doing. Our friends at Vila Isana were overjoyed to see us. They wanted to know how the army had treated us and how we had persuaded them to let us return. They wished us well as we made our way from the wide Negro river into the much narrower Isana River.

Jim and Skip Curtis were glad to see us as we stopped in their port. They were happy to have us back again in the work, although our stations were far apart. We told them about Edna's mother's serious illness and wondered what we should do.

Together we decided that Jim and Skip would join us for one month at our station to relieve me of all the work about the place so I could concentrate on completing the translation of the Baniwa New Testament. With only about three more months of translation work to be done, we hoped that maybe we might return to Canada to see Edna's mother before she passed on.

The Indian women were extremely glad to see us again. Some of them jumped up and down on the rocks for sheer joy. They had prayed continuously, trusting God to bring us back to them. There had been many reports from different sources saying we would never be back. The religious leader had taken it upon himself to urge the believers to take everything out of our house because we'd never return. Imagine, he encouraged them to break in and steal!

When old John, a dedicated believer from Tunui, realized what was happening, he went to our house, which was wide open by then, and removed the remaining stuff from our drawers, put them into a box and stored them in his own house. As soon as we arrived in Tunui he told me about the box of things he had saved for us. We thanked him profusely and asked him if we could pay him for it. "No," he said, "I did it for God." Our house was in shambles. Edna's accordion was still on the top bunk near the roof, where wind and weather had made a hole and rain had poured in and it was ruined. We moved in and cleaned up and got right back into translation work.

The people at a Nyengatu village had a different story. They told us they were harassed by the religious leader and his people. One church elder told us whenever the religious leader would stop at their village with a group of his students, he would send the women into their houses to gather all New Testaments and any other evangelical material, hide them under their shirts or dresses and sneak them to the boat. Those books were later on burned at the religious mission. This was confirmed by a non-Indian person working at the mission.

At one point when this harassment became so bad, a church elder told the SPI agent about it. The agent became so perturbed that he wrote the following letter.

MINISTRY OF AGRICULTURE
1st REGIONAL INSPECTORATE
Uaupes Agency

> The undersigned Commissioner of the Agency of the Society for the Protection of the Indian, in the Municipality of Uaupes and Ilha Grande, exercising the attributes on him bestowed by the law;

RESOLVES:

To entreat the Missionaries of the religious mission, pursuing their activities on the Isana River and its tributaries, when visiting the Indian villages where the majority or the entirety of its inhabitants are believers (Protestants) to avoid provoking disagreement with the Indian leaders and pastors who lead their brothers in the villages, in order not to cause animosity that might bring about unforseen consequences, which could force this Agency to assume vigorous measures against its perpetrators or instigators.

This petition is made in virtue of innumerable complaints that constantly arrive here in this Agency, made by various Indians who assert that they are always threatened and coerced by the above mentioned missionaries.

This Agency draws attention to the fact that freedom of religion in Brazil is free and guaranteed by the CONSTITUTION of the country, permitting the citizen, and equally the Indian, to follow or adopt the religion they chose.

Uaupes Agency of the Society for the Protection of the Indian, 5th day of April, 1961

(Signed) Athayde Ignacio Cardoso

As far as I know the above letter was never given to the religious leader involved. Similar offenses were not repeated.

The annual NTM mission conference, which we attended, was over and school was out. Our children were with us on the flight back to our jungle home.

As we were about to start the trip on our launch from the mouth of the Isana River to go to our station, we were interrupted by the arrival of a Gospel Recording technician wanting a ride with us to our tribe to do some recording.

Our launch was loaded with supplies for us and for our co-workers. Taking another person and his gear would make it quite crowded. Being a self-sufficient person he didn't mind, until his hammock rope came undone and he fell on the hard corner of a wooden box. After that he permitted me to tie his hammock ropes properly.

In one of the villages along the river we bought a live pig, tied it up on the stern of the boat and continued on. All went well until at night, when it started to rain. The pig tried to get into the warm motor room. It stumbled through the back door, which was open, and began to squeal as only a pig can. With a flashlight I could see the pig was caught, behind its front legs, in the well polished leather straps of the expensive recording equipment. It was hilarious!

When the owner of the equipment came to see what was so funny, he turned to us and said. "That's not one bit funny. That's my expensive recording equipment! Get the pig out of there."

In a few weeks he finished his recording and was ready to return. He wanted me to take him down river in the launch. I did not feel I could take off several weeks from the translation work to do that. The translation work might be finished in time for us to see Edna's mother before she passed on. I encouraged him to go down river by canoe. He could hire an Indian or two to take him. No, he didn't want that. He'd rather go alone. I provided him with a dugout canoe that would safely hold four people. I got him to tie his equipment to a seat, just in case the boat capsized. As soon as he started to go it became very evident that he didn't know how to paddle a canoe. But he kept on going. He got into a large eddy and began to drift in circles before the swift current took him down river again.

Several months later, we heard he had made it all the way to the mouth of the Isana River and on through the rocks near Uaupes. The Good Lord must have watched over him in a special way. We never heard from him again.

Antonio, my translation informant, who had been helping me while in Manaus, now begged me to let him go back to his people to teach them the things he had learned from the Bible. I was very reluctant to let him go but agreed he could go if he found another capable man who spoke the same dialect to help me.

The new informant was also named Antonio, but he was older than the first one. Madalena, his wife, just loved to sit quietly and listen to us as we discussed the Word and tried to put it into their language. Madalena came into the house to pray with Edna when our little Carol was so very sick. She had many black blotches on her face, arms and legs but they had cleared up since she took the strong antibiotic injections the State Health Department had left with us.

She loved to talk about the time when she first heard about the true and living God through her oldest son. Antonio, her husband, first heard the Gospel when he was working for a merchant on another river. He heard how his people were changing since they heard about the true and living God. He wanted to know more about this so he left his employment and returned to his people, heard the story of salvation and became a Christian.

Antonio loved to hear me discuss the Word before we wrote it down on paper. He said his heart was so full he could hardly take it any longer without sharing it with his own people. I begged him to stay until we were finished translating what was left to be done. I gave him permission to leave me but let him know how much it would help if he stayed. He and Madalena prayed about this and decided to help me until we were finished.

We had been listening to the commercial radio station every day at noon until the station went off the air due to some technical problem. We really wanted to get the message that might be sent to us about Edna's mother. God knew about this too. Finally, the day came when we finished the last verse in our translation. We were finished!

Antonio was all too glad to return to his people and share with them the precious truths he had learned as we worked on the translation. He left for his village immediately.

There were no people at our house that morning. The pressure was off and I had a headache. By noon it was so severe I told Edna I would lie down and not have lunch. I felt feverish and ached all over, just like malaria. I asked her to bring me the shortwave, battery operated radio and I would try to locate the commercial station on the dial.

There it was! They were giving messages on the radio again! The second message was for Edna informing her that her mother had passed away. Then there was static interference and I was unable to hear the date. It didn't really matter. What mattered was that we knew mother had passed away.

CHAPTER TWENTY-NINE

FURLOUGH -1963

It took nothing short of a high malaria fever to get me to listen to the radio at noon when we knew the station was off the air. But, it was on and I heard distinctly that Edna's mother had passed away. God knows how to direct His children. I immediately told Edna and the children who were home from boarding school. Together we rejoiced knowing that she was in the eternal presence of the Lord Jesus whom she loved.

Plans had been made to leave the station for furlough as soon as the translation work would be finished. This was July 1963 now and we were still far from Canada.

Our launch was at our station with us so we got it ready to make the long trip to Manaus from where we'd take a plane to Canada. The children were excited to go and begged me to take along their small dugout canoe, which had given them hours of fun and enjoyment. We took it but it was later blown off the boat during a storm and we never saw it again. The Indians, at Tunui, had a great time guiding the launch through the channel in the raging rapids. It certainly was much faster to go downstream than upstream, but the danger was proportionately greater. We stopped in each village to tell the folks we were going to Canada to see our families and about when we expected to be back. We decided, however, to pass by one of the villages where there was a bed of jagged rocks right in the port – until we saw a woman running frantically down the bank carrying a small box in her hand. She waved for us to stop. We couldn't ignore her. We carefully made our way through the maze of rocks till we reached the bank. She handed us a cardboard box. The folks from down river had sent it to be relayed from village to village until it would reach us. In the box we found our mail for the last several months, and there was the telegram from Edna's brother telling us mother had died the 19th of June.

All along the river the Indians were sad to see us leave but we assured them we'd be back again. There were other missionaries to help them in many ways although there was no one who was able to teach them the Word of God in their own language. While we were gone, the church elders took their responsibilities seriously. They called the believers together every evening for a time of singing and reading God's Word, teaching them as well as they knew how.

Furlough in Canada was a wonderful time for renewing acquaintances, reporting to supporting churches and visiting in homes of friends. While on furlough I spent as much time as possible checking my translation work. After each book of the New Testament was finished, I photocopied it, ready to be sent to the printing press in Brazil.

Malaria hit me on a cold, stormy day in March, despite the fact that it is a tropical disease. Fortunately, our family doctor had spent some time in a tropical country and knew how to treat and eradicate malaria. The lab technician at the local hospital was from Guyana and was well acquainted with malaria, spotted it in my blood right away. Our doctor did such a good job of treating me that the dreaded disease never returned. While I lay in bed, sweating out the fever, with the radio on, I heard the news that John F. Kennedy, president of the United States, had been assassinated.

Time went by fast, and before long it was time to return to Brazil. This time we left Audrey and Joanne with my oldest sister so they could continue their studies in Canada. Audrey prepared to go into nursing and Joanne to finish high school. The separation was painful but we knew it was for the best.

CHAPTER THIRTY

NEW TESTAMENT

The Baniwa New Testament was to be printed in NTM's print shop at Puraquequara, the mission's base on the banks of the Amazon River. The printer believed he could do it, although he had never done a job like that in such humid, tropical conditions. He had been getting equipment and materials ready for some time. He had a special plate maker which used electricity to burn the image of the type-written pages on the plates. There were times when there was no electric power, so he put the plates on top of the print shop roof to be burned by the blistering sun. He was experimenting because, apparently, this method had never been tried before. Under normal circumstances it worked fine, but when a cloud suddenly appeared, the heat from the sun diminished and the plates didn't burn well. Sometimes a cloud brought not only shade but a sudden burst of rain. There were many obstacles to be overcome. Among them was the damp paper crumpling up while going through the Gestetner printer.

Slowly the 620 page books were being printed. Then they were bound and packaged for shipment to the Isana River. The Baniwas were very glad to receive the New Testament written in their own language. Until now they had been using the Curipaco New Testament translated by Sophie Muller in Colombia. The Baniwa people could understand the Curipaco language but it was quite different, and the translation had a question after each verse to be answered by the readers. Now they had their own but without the questions. Some were not so sure it really was theirs, because it wasn't in their particular dialect. There were seven different dialects among the Baniwas, so we had chosen the one with the most speakers in it. Not every clan could be pleased.

The Baniwa New Testament had the distinction of being the first complete New Testament ever printed in an Indian language in Brazil .

The churches grew in faith as time went on. Those on the Colombian border enjoyed an occasional visit from Sophie Muller, their first missionary. We made it a point to meet with her there whenever possible. One of these visits occurred on the border on the Cuiari River in a small village named Mouth of the Iyana Creek. In our small boat and outboard motor it was within one day's travel from our station. We had packed up the children, some food, trade goods, some simple medicines and were on our way. Of course, we took an Indian guide along.

The river was quite low and many rocks stuck their jagged heads out of the black water. The children enjoyed watching the kingfishers flying ahead of us from tree to tree waiting till we got nearby before they flew away again. In the distance the thunderbird called in response to the noise of the outboard motor. Later on we named one of our larger canoes *KOYOLIPA*, which is thunderbird in Baniwa.

The village was small, less than half a dozen mud huts. We were given an empty room to stay in while Sophie Muller had her hammock hanging in a new shelter the Indians had put up just for her. There she sat and worked. She either translated or wrote up new choruses for them to sing in any one of the many languages she had learned. No idle moments in her life!

It was the beginning of the rainy season and it rained every day. With it came the frogs, croaking merrily in the rising water along the banks of the rivers. The men and boys arose as early as possible each morning to catch as many frogs as they could for food.

The fog was still hanging low when we heard the clanging of the makeshift bell calling everyone to breakfast. On the high table in the middle of the village were numerous blackened pots, some containing frogs, others fresh fish. I decided to try fresh frogs that morning since I had never eaten frogs before. The elder prayed thanking God for the frogs and fish in the pots, for the manioc bread on the table and the manioc flour drink.

As he said his "amen", the men dug with their calloused hands into the cauldrons of frogs, grabbed one at a time and bit into its swollen stomach to slurp out the eggs, laid the carcass aside and went for another, and another. My appetite for frogs was gone! I decided to have fish instead.

Later on, Sophie Muller told us that she admired us for eating with the Indians. She didn't eat with them but had them bring her food into her shelter

With our children in the missionary children's school Edna and I spent about half of our time traveling from village to village teaching the Christians. We saw the need to teach more about salvation by grace without any works. Often when I'd ask them how they were saved they responded by saying, "by leaving witchcraft, by doing good, by attending church services," and so on.

Repeatedly I explained to them how Father God together with His Son decided He would take upon Himself the sin of all the people on earth and die on the cross so that everyone who would believe in Jesus would have eternal life freely. After hearing this again they would respond and say that only Jesus Christ could save them because he died to pay for their sins on the cross. It was their own idea to go and write this on the huge boulders in the river for people to see as they paddled by in their canoes. They wrote *APADATSA CRISTO* - only Christ, in huge white letters on the flat faces of the rocks. They wanted all their friends, saved and unsaved, to get the message that only Jesus could save people from their sin and fear of death.

On one trip of over two months I taught one hundred and thirteen sessions and most of the time it was on the completed work of Christ on the cross of Calvary.

The church had the New Testament in their language and was growing. There were those who went out to teach unreached areas of their own people and some went to other tribes.

Antonio Cubeu was a faithful believer. His mother was from the Cubeu tribe so he knew her language. He decided to share the gospel with her people. Several men volunteered to join him in his undertaking. As they went through the jungles on a little used trail covered with moss, slime and dead leaves hiding the protruding roots, a deadly snake bit Antonio in the leg. What should they do? Should they return to their village? No. They decided to remain right where they were and ask God to heal him and then they would continue. They prayed for Antonio's healing. Then they found some jungle plants they customarily used for snake bites and applied them to the swelling foot.

After building a temporary shelter of palm leaves the men spent much time reading the New Testament together and talking about its meaning. They sang and prayed. Several went out to hunt while the others stayed with Antonio. These men together believed God for recovery and before too many days they were on their way to the unreached people with the good news of salvation. God had protected them just as He said He would.

Aprigio Lino, who has been mentioned earlier, was a fervent Curipaco believer, living on the upper Isana River near the Colombian border. He knew the Nyengatu, Portuguese and Spanish languages quite well and wanted to serve God. During a Bible conference he offered to go and evangelize on the upper Uaupes river for a few months. He took several other believers with him. He was faithful in sharing the Word of God wherever he stopped along the river. The people of that tribe were somewhat wary of the Gospel and did not readily accept his visits. But, he talked to them and gave them his personal testimony of how he had found peace when he believed in Jesus Christ as Lord and Savior.

This suspicion was evident in all the smaller villages until he arrived at another larger village where the leaders did not want any evangelical to be in their homes. They did not invite him in but rather beat him up and sent him on his way. It was in this village where a man by name of Arcanjo became a Christian. His life changed so much the other Indians noticed it and began to see that Jesus had made a difference in his life. They became more tolerant of his faith but were not willing to become believers themselves.

Some years later he wrote the following letter to missionary Paulo Carrenho.

Greetings in the name of our Lord Jesus!

My name is Joao Arcanjo and I live in Miriti Punta. I'm writing to you my missionary friend Paulo Carrenho.

I put my trust in God a long time ago and continue in the faith. I live on the Caiari River among those who do not want the Word of God. I am the only believer among my friends and relatives and am persecuted a lot, even by Father Roberto, from Iauarate. He threatens to kick me out of my own house if I continue to tell other people the Word of God. On two occasions he told me he did not want me to stay here among the people of the religious mission, not even for a short time. I told him I was not going to leave my own property. Then he became very angry with me and they burned down my house which made me very sad.

I'm writing this letter to inform you so you can talk to the authorities and have them remove this hateful person.

Two men from my village complained about me to the religious leader, so I beg you to persuade the governmental authorities to have this man removed.

Please pray for Antonio Barbosa and me that we will remain faithful and not permit the devil to deceive us.

Greetings to all the believers in Manaus and ask them to pray for us.

Joao Arcanjo, Miriti Punta.

CHAPTER THIRTY-ONE

EDNA'S SNAKE STORIES

One day while I was writing this book, Edna came up with the following chapter on snakes:

I hate snakes. They strike, they kill, they sneak into dark corners and maybe into the thatch roof. Yes, they scare me. Just thinking about them might give me a nightmare. No, they are not at all beautiful the way God created them. And no doubt it is because of the tragic deception he created in the hearts of Adam and Eve, that we treat snakes like our real enemy. Enemies they are, as they strike many who are not cautious, or unaware of the danger hidden in unlikely places. In the jungles they may hide under leaves, or in trees, or under logs. Our numerous experiences took place in the jungles of Brazil. Snakes are always ready to strike.

The river became our high way, the dugout canoe our vehicle. Our night lodging often became some abandoned thatch roof over poles, or partially broken down mud hut. However, any small shelter was welcome for protection from the tropical rain storms that approached without warning. One particular night we found just that. We struggled through forest brush and in the semi-darkness noticed a broken down shelter. Yes, it was ample for stringing four hammocks: one for our three year old son, another for our Indian guide and two for my husband and myself. It took a while for me to settle down. Henry and Jimmy were already in the world of blissful slumber, while I was rolling around in my hammock trying to find the just-right position. Finally I too was ready for that comfortable sleep. What was that I heard? Sounded like a tiger was sniffing around for food. Yes, I thought I heard his breathing. He soon disappeared. Praying to God again for protection, I too slept. But not for long! From Henry's hammock came a sleepy groan. Was I hearing right? He muttered that a snake was in his hammock. Yes, near his throat. I became paralyzed with fright. A thousand miles from a doctor, no phone, nowhere to go for help. Here we were in the jungle, how could Jimmy and I cope with something as terrible as a snake bite in the middle of the night? I called our guide Francisco who was in a very deep sleep. He answered with a groan. I told him to go quickly and help fight a snake in Henry's hammock. Slowly he came to a sitting position in the hammock, bowed his head and began to pray. I quickly reminded him that now it was time to get up and help Henry. Slowly, and no doubt terribly afraid, he approached the hammock. Cautiously, he started looking for that deadly creature. Henry reminded him it was around his neck. Praise be, this was only a dream!

How well I remember our small, mud floor, thatched roof bedroom at Seringa Ropita. The place itself was beautiful and restful. The clean black river had become our swimming pool, bath tub, washing machine and our highway. The high tree-covered hill on the opposite side was rising majestically out of the jungle floor. We soon discovered we were not the only creation enjoying this jungle area. There were snakes of every description.

One beautiful and sunny morning I went down to the river to wash clothes. Henry was already busy with his translation in a nearby building. Our four children had added just enough clothes to the pile on the floor to merit a trip to the river for a quiet and relaxing time on the rock. I was bending down to pick up the clothes when my fingers touched a very frightened snake. It is so good to have a husband at close call. However, by the time he was there, the snake had escaped!

Another evening the family was gathered around the table waiting for supper. I was about to put the food on the table, when a good-sized snake stuck out his tongue trying to sneak away from behind the stove to a safer hiding place.

Probably one of my scariest moments was one dark, quiet night when Henry was out traveling. The children were home from boarding school. They were tucked into bed and sound asleep. The flashlight, as usual, was slipped under the mattress for an easy grab. It was very common for a bat to swish over our heads in the dead of the night. And of course there could be a snake. The cat was curled up on the floor in the kitchen. I had dozed off into a light sleep, but was soon aroused by the cat chasing a snake around the bed. With the small flashlight I saw, not only the cat, but also a snake trying to hide under a piece of furniture. I warily followed the commotion to the next room praying it would not go into the room where our children were sleeping. I wanted to call an Indian in from the nearby village to the kill the snake. No, it was too far to run, and maybe there was more danger lurking in the dark path to the village. I prayed and did what I hated most, grabbed the machete which was always within grabbing distance. Cautiously, but quickly, I cut the snake in the middle. I was really proud of myself and could not wait to tell my husband.

Late afternoons were always a time to look forward to. After a hot, humid and tiring day, we would change into our bathing suits, gather the soiled clothes of the day and make our way down the bank and onto a huge, smooth rock. Out came the soap and with feet comfortably cooling in the running water, the suds started floating away in the river like fluffy clouds. One day I was enjoying the quiet, cool moments. I was suddenly aroused by a strange feeling coming out of the suds up my leg. A deadly red, black and white necklace-like coral snake cautiously moved up my leg. Oh Lord, now what do I do? Should I shake it off, strike it with my hand, or just wait and see what could happen. It stopped and looked right into my eyes. Then up it started again. The closer to my heart it would strike the quicker I would die. I whipped it off with my hand! Frightened, it quickly slipped back into the water. God had once again reminded me of His promise in Psalm 91. Only later did I scream! My husband heard the blood-curdling scream. "What's wrong?" He called from the work shop on top of the hill. I had been unable to scream before, so now it was a delayed reaction!

Our three daughters were home for a four month school break. They enjoyed the river and the beautiful sand beaches a lot. We planned a few weeks of traveling from village to village along the Isana River. We had a lot of fun singing and watching for birds, monkeys, or the beautiful orchids often seen growing from the trees along the jungle edge . Peacefully our boat sliced through the black waters. Of course the unpleasant memories are the dangerous rocks hidden just under the water, the boiling rapids we had to cross and the tropical storms that could so suddenly make traveling hazardous. And sometimes we saw a snake swimming right next to the canoe. This particular trip had been extra strenuous. We had arrived at a village, were greeted warmly by the people and then had to make a decision. Should I and the children cross the dangerous rapids with the men, or walk through the jungles with some of the Indian women. We chose the latter. The kids and I enjoyed our walk through the jungle. Soon we were very tired, hot and thankful to arrive in the Indian village. We felt welcome and were soon taken to a thatch roof shelter.

The men had not yet arrived and it was getting dark. What a relief when we heard the noise of a motor! Thankfully Henry and the Indians had safely crossed the rapids. They had struggled through the angry rapids and were very tired. The Christian Indians had begun to construct a building for worship. The sticks had formed a wall waiting for mud to make a solid wall. The palm leaf roof had already made a lovely shelter from the rains. Quickly our hammocks were strung up between some poles. Already the Indians had "benches" from logs they had cut in the jungle. This was to become our home for the coming days. Our tired bodies soon brought sleep to all but for me. I heard the thunder rolling in, lightening was already streaking across the sky. Soon all were awake. The children's hammocks had to be moved to the center where the rain would not reach them. And again the children went to sleep, but Henry and I were awake. Henry soon had his eyes focused on a large snake coming in for shelter from the storm. Surely it would just decide to crawl through the building and out the other side. He waited. His hammock had been tied too low, almost resting on the log bench under his body. Unbelievably, the snake came right for his hammock and settled down right under him. He remembered the shells in his pants' pocket hanging on a pole in the far corner. The gun also was too far away. The gun was a way of protection from wild game and especially snakes.

I was aroused, unaware of what was happening. My eyes turned towards Henry's hammock. The little flame of the small lantern shed enough light for me to see this huge snake strung out under Henry's hammock. I was paralyzed! If I called, it may rouse my husband to the point where it would frighten the snake. Maybe he was still sleeping. I had to make a quick decision.

However, Henry was awake and quietly chinned up the rope of his hammock, and jumped away. He called Julio, our Indian guide, who was sleeping in a hut nearby. God had kept him awake too. He was there in seconds. Henry had already picked up his machete. But at a glance Julio noticed this was a very poisonous snake and was capable of jumping a distance. Julio knew a machete was too short so he grabbed a long pole out of the wall and quickly struck and broke its back. He then dragged it out and let it be. The ants might even have dragged it away by morning. We now settled down in our hammocks and slept.

Morning came. The sun was already pouring its heat on us at six o'clock. An Indian, John the Baptist, stood near the snake. He was praying. We quickly rolled out of our hammocks and joined him. He asked, "Did you visit the witch doctor down river yesterday?"

"Yes we did."

"Do you realize he threw a curse on you? The curse is a snake." Oh yes, we have heard that this happens. John the Baptist said that again this was proof that God's power far exceeds Satan's power. Our faith in God's power and protection had been strengthened. Great is God's faithfulness!

The Baniwa Indians were very organized in their way. Every six months the Christian believers would plan a conference for all who wished to attend. The surrounding Indian villages were invited. Each brought his hammock, and a lot of smoked wild meat which they had smoked for this occasion. They invited us to teach. In advance they had built a small shelter for us. In this particular village the thatch roof shelter was big enough to hang three hammocks, a place for our grey box which contained a lot of worm medicine, trading goods and a few personal items. This was a special four days of Bible conference.

The Indians called us at two o'clock one night telling us they saw the strange star with a tail! It was a comet. After these days of wonderful fellowship it was time to take down our hammocks and be on our way to the next village. Our thatched roof was held up with poles on either side just about a foot from the hanging hammock. Taking down the hammock we noticed a five feet long snake which apparently had shared our cozy hut maybe for as long as we had been there. I was ever so thankful it had not tried to share my hammock too! I ran out as fast as I could. An Indian noticed it and came with his machete and killed it!

Edna found a snake in this shelter.

Soon we took our baggage down the hill where our small boat was bouncing in shallow water. We were standing in ankle deep water loading the boat. An Indian came beside me and swiftly jerked me away from the boat. Near my feet, under the water, was a large snake curled up, far too close for comfort. Again God had protected.

I must record just one more experience . This one particular time we took Jimmy and Arlene with us as we wound our way to Manaus where our three children were attending school about 1000 miles from our jungle home. After a long day of traveling we were tired, and arranged to stop with friends for the night. Arlene, then five years old, decided to explore an old building on the yard. I went to check on her, and all but stopped breathing. She was pushing a long snake from its sleeping position to see if it was dead! The snake was very much alive and starting to chase her. Fortunately, the frog in its mouth kept it from striking. God is good!

Time after time we saw God protect us and our children. They, too, had times when it was obvious the angels were surrounding them. We look back on these experiences, as a reminder of God's wonderful protection as stated in Psalm 91:13. "He will command the angels to guard you in all your ways. You will tread upon the lion and the cobra - you will trample the great lion and the serpent. Because he loves you He will rescue you."

CHAPTER THIRTY-TWO

NYENGATU PEOPLE

Through the years I had been studying the Nyengatu language. Joaquim and Dominga, who lived next door, spoke mostly Nyengatu in their home. He was a Baniwa and she a Nyengatu. Since he knew her language and she didn't care to speak his, they always spoke Nyengatu although she understood Baniwa and spoke it much better than we did.

I had been asking him to teach me Nyengatu, and before long he helped me to translate portions of the New Testament into Nyengatu. I discovered that the grammar of the language was very similar to the Baniwa grammar. In many cases prefixes and affixes, even infixes, were in the same position in both languages. The words, however, were completely different.

During one of my frequent trips down to the mouth of the Isana River to pick up our mail and any supplies that might have arrived, I stopped at a large Nyengatu village called Dog Fish Village. They heard me and came running down to the riverbank to greet me.

"Come on up and eat with us," the leader invited me. I joined them in their mud house. There was a bamboo slat wall between this room and the next one where the women ate. The men were sitting on a large mat on which were several earthen pots containing small fish seasoned with a liberal amount of fiery hot peppers. They dipped their manioc bread into this and carefully put it into their mouths without touching the lips. If they did, it would burn there for a long time.

Believing I didn't understand their language, they talked about me. "Ariki eats with us and likes our food. All the other white men coming to us eat on their own. They don't like our food." I was deeply moved when I heard them say these things and I realized how much they appreciated it when we missionaries ate with them.

God impressed upon us the need to get the whole New Testament translated into the Nyengatu language. I shared this conviction with the rest of the workers and with mission leadership. They decided I should move into Nyengatu territory to improve my knowledge of the language and translate the New Testament. After moving down to the mouth of the river where there were many Nyengatu speaking Indians, we spent much time studying the language.

Henry and informant Julio translating.

A Brazilian couple came to replace us among the Baniwa people. Paulo and Eglacy and their small daughter, Claudia, were very dear people. They had a deep love for the Indians and a desire to learn the language and teach them. Paulo, raised in the city of Sao Paulo, was a school teacher. Eglacy was raised in the city of Manaus and was a nurse.

The day Paulo and Eglacy arrived at the mouth of the Isana River, on the amphibious commercial plane, my brother-in-law, Herb Penner, and his pastor, Art Neufeld, arrived also. They came to visit us. Herb and his wife, Martha, had been supporting us in our ministry from the beginning and he wanted to see, first hand, what we were doing.

Herb and Art shared a room in our house and enjoyed spending time in hammocks just to rest and read. They both loved to eat the fresh fish Edna fried but Herb wasn't too keen about eating turtle. A young fellow from the village next door invited them to go fishing with him. He caught several good sized wide-mouthed bass, but Herb and Art caught nothing.

Their enjoyment was cut short when one morning we heard on the news that the airline making the bimonthly stops at the mouth of the Isana River had gone bankrupt. Then an announcement was made that another airline would pick up all the passengers who had return tickets to Manaus.

I took them down to Vila Isana to wait for the plane, but no plane came. Later we heard on the news that a Brazilian Air Force plane would pick up all stranded passengers. That didn't materialize either. Needless to say, Herb was becoming quite anxious when he realized he was stuck in the jungles without any way out. He was supposed to attend an important meeting at home by the end of the month, and here he was 800 miles from Manaus and no way to get there. Art didn't have any special deadline, so was quite relaxed and enjoyed himself.

Since Herb was so anxious to attend the meeting at the end of the month we took him and Art to the nearest town, some seventy-five kilometers away, to see if there was any possibility of getting on a plane to Manaus. Nobody knew about any plane coming within a week. But there was a river boat in the port getting loaded for its monthly trip to Manaus that could take them there in five days.

There was a problem, however, neither one of them knew any Portuguese and nobody on the boat spoke English. We discussed this with the owner of the boat and he was more than willing to take them down to Manaus as fast as he could. We told him the men had airline tickets to leave Manaus in six days and he promised to have the men there in time.

The trip turned out to be quite interesting considering the fact that they were unable to communicate with anyone. There was plenty of food on board and they ate well. There was dried, salted beef, fish and turtle. Herb already knew what turtle looked like so he wouldn't take any. There was always the faithful standby of rice and beans.

It was a few months later we heard they had arrived in Manaus in the early hours of the day their plane was to leave. The boat owner himself took them to the Mission Home by car. From there they called a taxi and hurried off to the airport and were able get on board the plane on their way back to Canada.

Paulo and his wife had stayed with us, among the Nyengatu people, for over two weeks. They had picked up some phrases from the songs and choruses they sang in the services. Paulo's keen desire to speak with the people was evident when we took the family to their assignment several days travel upriver.

Traveling along steadily in the loaded canoe, we stopped wherever there were people. At one small shelter near a garden they waved us in. A young girl was sick and they wanted some help from us. While Eglacy, the nurse, and Edna discussed the situation Paulo stood at the sick girl's hammock repeatedly saying, *"Cristo roui opoderi, Cristo roui opoderi,"* which translated is: The blood of Christ is able. Those were the only words he could speak in her language and he used them.

Paulo felt an urgency to learn to speak with the people in order to teach them. So, he applied himself to learning the language and before long he was able to teach to his heart's content. It wasn't easy for them to learn the Indians' culture and ways. We introduced them to a Baniwa Bible conference just a few days after helping them settle in their first home among the Baniwas. The Indians were very happy they had come to live with them. They helped them in every way they could.

We accompanied them to Tunui to attend the Bible conference. There a large building had recently been built for meetings and eating. It also was to accommodate many of the visitors that were coming. There were a number of temporary palm frond shelters for more visitors. Meetings were held in the large, new building where there were row after row of roughly hewn logs for seats. The walls were fences made of thin saplings to allow air to circulate and to keep the dogs out.

Prayer meetings began long before dawn. The men met in one place and the women in another. However, some of the women were preparing breakfast. When prayer meeting was over the men all went down to the river for their morning dip. Paulo and I joined them and took the opportunity to shave. We had to hurry up and follow them up the steep rocky steps back to the village.

When Paulo and I appeared, they were all gathered in the center of the village holding their bowls in their hands. High tables groaned with the load of dozens of blackened pots, full of boiled manioc flour gruel, some seasoned with salt, some without, others with hot peppers. After reciting verses, singing some choruses and a prayer, the gruel was dished out to each person. I had already learned to ask for the gruel with salt in it. Paulo was served from the bland gruel and he became convinced he'd not be there for breakfast again. So, the next morning he took his time while shaving and suggested I go on up ahead and he'd follow. We shouldn't wait for him. He did take his time and arrived in the village square after everyone had finished and everything had been cleared up.

But, there was Madalena – a sensitive, caring woman – who had noticed that Paulo wasn't there. She had poured all the leftovers together into one pot and was ready, with a smile, to serve him when he came walking into the village square!

He turned to me and asked, "What shall I do?"

"You have no choice, Paulo, if you want to please her, you'll have to take it," was my reply.

He never again appeared late for their breakfast. He would take the gruel of his choice.

Before we returned to our translation work at the mouth of the river, we decided we would meet half way between our two stations for the next conference. This would take place in a few months.

Several months later Paulo appeared in the village, without his wife or child, with some believers from a nearby village. We both enjoyed each other's fellowship. We had not seen each other for quite some time.

Prayer meeting began before dawn. The men gathered in one place and the women in another. I recognized each believer's voice as they prayed, one after the other. Then there came a voice I didn't recognize. The person prayed a few sentences in Baniwa, then slipped into Portuguese. I realized it was Paulo. He had used all the Baniwa words he knew, then reverted into his mother tongue. Paulo was a very good missionary, he related to the people well and learned to speak their language quickly.

After some time there Paulo and Eglacy decided they could have a greater ministry with the people if they spent more time in their villages teaching them right in their homes. Leaving the comfort of their house, they moved into whatever room given to them by the people of each village. They enjoyed it, and accepted the challenge of teaching the children to read and write during the day and at night they taught Bible.

They were careful to keep young Claudia in good health and got a laying hen from the Indians. She made her a nest right in their room where she laid an egg a day for a long time. They gave the egg to their baby. When the eggs became fewer, they gave the hen extra care and food; and soon she laid an egg a day again.

It was easy enough to get eggs there in the village but impossible to obtain powdered milk. They were getting very low and Eglacy prayed fervently to God asking Him to, somehow, supply the needed milk for their small child. The day the milk was completely gone she knelt down beside the baby's hammock and entreated God to do a miracle of some sort and supply milk for her Claudia.

Having cast her care upon Him, who alone was able to do the impossible, she arose confidently and went to teach a class of children.

Later on that same day, a trader stopped at the village and delivered a cardboard box to them. In it was a five pound can of powdered whole milk. How she praised God for answering her prayer! In fact, God had been answering that prayer many days earlier. While this trader was doing business with the people of the nearby village, Edna and I made up a package of food stuff, including a can of powdered milk for Paulo and Eglacy to send to them with the trader.

We were not aware they were low on powdered milk, but God knew and He impressed this upon our minds. Later on when we heard how desperate Eglacy had been we were ever so thankful we had been obedient to God.

CHAPTER THIRTY-THREE

CHURCH GROWTH

Paulo and Eglacy were teaching the Baniwas from village to village in one area while Anne Golias and Elpidia Pinheiro were doing the same farther upriver. Alma Egeland was teaching among the Nyengatu people in the lower regions of the Isana River. There were times when progress seemed very slow, but they kept on teaching. Before long the young students began to use Portuguese much more freely.

Paulo, Eglacy and family with friends.

Most of the parents were very anxious to have their children learn the Portuguese language and to understand arithmetic. They had been cheated many a time by unscrupulous traders just because they didn't know how to calculate.

The Indians, especially those farther up river, were so desirous of having a permanent teacher in their villages that they built school houses. We discovered this on one of our trips into the area. Unfortunately, it was impossible to make use of all of these new buildings for the lack of teachers. Consequently, many of the buildings fell into disrepair. As time went by it was noticed that some of the more aggressive students were capable of teaching the younger ones. Their talents were put to use, and many made good progress in school.

Joan Wood joined forces to teach among the Nyengatu people and she saw right away that the only way to be able to teach in all the villages was to prepare the natives themselves to teach their own people. The ideal

171

would be to give them enough education so they could become primary school teachers to their own people, paid by the local municipality.

This possibility was investigated and we were informed all we needed was a qualified school teacher to take them through the first five years of studies, and then they could become primary school teachers.

This need was made known to missionary candidates, and soon Adauta, a qualified teacher, joined our ranks. She invited those who had already received four years of schooling to return to get one more year so they could become teachers in their own villages. After some time she supervised more than a dozen schools she had organized on the lower Isana River where the natives themselves taught their own children.

Meanwhile Hazel Bathke and Walkiria A. de Souza, in the upper regions of the river, were steadfast in their teaching ministry. Jim and Skip Curtis[1] were having a spiritual ministry among the Baniwas and their nearby Curipaco neighbors. Fortunately, there were several large villages nearby, and the attendance was sufficient for two teachers. They not only taught in school but also gave medical help to those who came for it. They were kept very busy.

In 1965 our four children were all going to boarding school in Puraquequara - PQQ, near Manaus. We had our last breakfast before taking them to catch the amphibious plane to Manaus to start another school year. Arlene prayed at the table, not just thanking God for the food, but – "Please God, help Mommy to have another baby!"

God had it all planned. Yes, we needed and wanted another baby. And, after the kids were gone we packed a bit of food, our hammocks and started the motor and in our small canoe started a winding trip to visit many of the Baniwa people up and down the river where they were anxiously waiting to learn more of God's love and care. Paulo and Eglacy Carrenho joined us in a village where they had already prepared for a short Bible conference. Edna and Eglacy had much in common – both were expecting an addition to the family.

We began to make plans. Our children at PQQ were excited and could hardly wait. Macon Hare, field chairman, had already made plans to invite us to go to Manaus to take his place as mission leader for the West Brazil field. Eglacy and Edna would take the plane to Manaus, while Paulo and I would finish some work and follow later on by boat. We all had to be there for our annual mission conference starting May 16th, 1966.

We took them to Sao Gabriel da Cachoeira where we all got into an old dilapidated truck. The door had to be closed with wire. The ladies sat in the front seat and Paulo and I got on the back.

172

The 19th was the special day marked on the calendar. I went to PQQ to head up the conference. Adele Emsheimer stayed with Edna in Manaus, and took care of the Mission Home during the time of conference, at Puraquequara, PQQ.

Edna felt fine. In fact she had good health all the way through the pregnancy. It was the 19th but no sign of that being the day! She lay in her hammock and heard Ted Emsheimer had just arrived to get the mail and would be going right back. He asked, "Do you want to send a message to Henry?"

"No, not really, all is well." Then on second thought she said she would go to a walk-in clinic to see how things were coming. The nurses who examined her seemed puzzled. "No pain?" they asked.

"No, I'm feeling fine." Not all seemed right though. "You must immediately go to the hospital. The baby will be born very soon."

She smiled. Boy, that would be easy! I couldn't be there – Adele was in charge now. Edna really appreciated her concern, and Ted would tell me to come right away. Well, maybe in two or three hours! Ted delivered her verbal message that she would have the baby right away. No, there was no pain. In that case, she thought, it would be another 10 or more hours! I quickly finished my work at the conference and then made my way back to Manaus and the Mission Home. I got myself ready, bought a bouquet of flowers and was on my way to the maternity ward at Santa Casa.

At the time I was getting myself ready, Dr. Gesta got Edna ready!

"When will the baby be born?" Edna asked the doctor who seemed to be impatient and concerned. "NOW," he said! Edna was on the delivery table, Adele was there too.

"You have a baby girl," the nurse said.

Henry holding new daughter.

I needed to go back to PQQ to take care of some matters at conference and would return the next day and bring our children along. Edna was feeling really good, and the baby was fine. Audrey arrived in Manaus from PQQ in time to join Adele to get Edna from the hospital by taxi. The rest of the children stayed at PQQ with me. The next day Joanne, Arlene and Jimmy were admiring Luanne, their new sister.

Then leadership asked us to take care of the high school dormitory the following school year. So we moved to Puraquequara.

In due time Paulo and Eglacy returned to the Isana River to continue their ministry there. But Edna and I were asked to remain to help out in the school and administration. During that time we were able to make yearly visits to the Baniwa people to teach and encourage them. On those trips I worked at revising the Baniwa New Testament with the help of the believers.

Jim Curtis had made a small airstrip near their mission station so MAF - Mission Aviation Fellowship could bring them supplies and provide means of transportation to and from Manaus. This was a tremendous blessing to everyone involved. Several very sick young men were flown to Manaus for medical help who later returned in good health.

Some of the Baniwa students enrolled in an Agricultural College in Manaus, where they also finished their high-school training. Later on one of them took a three-year Bible course in Manaus. Another became very active in native governmental affairs.

Others continued on in their tribal areas to raise their own families. One of them wrote a very touching letter to Hazel telling her how much she had helped him in his life. Here are parts of it:

Greetings in the name of Jesus our Lord and Savior!

Dear Mother in the faith,

It gives me the utmost joy and satisfaction to write you this small letter just to inform you how I'm doing here on the Isana.

But, first I want to ask for your forgiveness for not having written sooner. It is not that I didn't want to, but because of the great distance where I live, you know how it is, don't you, – Mom?

Hazel, I think your prayers for me were so powerful that I ended up finding a help-meet among the Curipacos. I'm very happy for this.

Hazel, I would so much love to see you and talk with you personally.

[1] Skip mentions this in her book: Though the Waters Roar

Another thing Hazel, I want to thank you first for your prayers. I ask you to continue to pray for me, asking that God will give me steadfastness in His Word and in the faith.

Attentively, your son in the faith,
Raul Feliciano M. Brazao

Another one of her students also wrote a letter of gratitude.

Dear Teacher Hazel,

I'm writing you this letter with much love from the bottom of my heart. Hazel, the main reason for me to write you this letter is to thank you for all your effort in teaching me to read and to write. I know I made it very hard for you, but, thank God, you succeeded to teach me to be what I should be. Today I have a wife and three children, one daughter and two sons, and I am very happy with my children. If it hadn't been for you what would I be today? I wouldn't be anything in this world. I remember everything you taught me, I remember all the Bible verses and for this I want to thank you with all my heart. It is too bad that you are so far away that I can't ever talk with you, but I will never forget you.

Many greetings!
Irineu Laureano Rodrigues

Prospectors who had been searching for mineral deposits in our area found gold dust in the sand beach just below the turbulent rapids at Uaupes. It wasn't long before the place was overrun with men panning for gold. Some of the believing Baniwas and Nyengatus caught the fever and were digging as eagerly as anybody. They didn't earn much more than minimum wages unless they worked very long days.

Among the many items the believing Indians wanted to buy were small, battery operated, transistor radios. We were disappointed, to say the least, at their desire for such unnecessary goods. But what could we do? It was their money and they could spend it as they wished. We would have preferred they bought more practical things for their families.

More gold was found within Baniwa territory. Prospectors moved in and developed the area for the natives to begin working. Soon there was a migration to that area. They would go for several weeks at a time and then return with enough money to do some shopping. The believers were frustrated with the ungodly life style of many of the outsiders.

Just prior to returning to Canada, in 1985, I had spent several weeks teaching the Baniwas while distributing new copies of the Baniwa New Testament which had just arrived from the printers. On the way to the tribal area I traveled on a commercial river boat that was pushing two barges containing 150 tonnes of fuel upstream to the army base.

As the boat was navigating the turbulent rapids of the upper Negro River, it got hung up on a submerged rock and began to tip dangerously while the swift current pushed against the side of the bow threatening to turn it over. The pilot of the boat tried his best to manoeuver the vessel out of danger, while the owner of the boat yelled at me above the noise of the powerful motor, to get into an aluminum boat tied to the stern. I quickly grabbed my brief case with all my documents and jumped into the boat leaving the hundreds of Baniwa New Testaments on board. It seemed like the enemy of our souls did not want these new copies of the New Testament to be distributed to the believers. Within an hour the boat was free and I boarded again and the trip continued on slowly for several hours, only to be stranded again, on a huge, flat rock submerged in quiet water. All the weight of the two barges shoved them far upon the hidden boulder making it extremely difficult to extricate them. The men went in two canoes to the riverbank, cut down six trees in the jungles and used them as levers to pry the barges off the rocks. It took several hours of hard work to free them. Finally we were on the way again.

The Baniwas were so hungry for more Bible teaching in their own language, it was hard for me to think I might be leaving them for good. I told them I would soon be going to Canada and my future was in God's hands. At each village they received me with enthusiasm and served me with special drinks made of the purple *assai* palm nuts, or bananas squashed into a drink. At mealtime they would serve me the portions of meat they knew I liked. There were always those clinging to me who wanted to know more about the Word of God.

The Baniwas gathered in the evening in their chapels. The elders sitting on high seats in front of the congregation called me up to talk to the people. I taught them the importance of the Word of God in their lives and the need for reading and studying it. I suggested they should do like Paul told Timothy to do in 2 Timothy 2:15, Study to show yourself approved unto God, a workman that needs not to be ashamed, rightly dividing the word of truth.

Then I called the leading elder to come and receive his new copy of the New Testament in his own language. I explained to them that I did not have enough books for each one of them so I would give them only to the elders but that the rest of them would receive them as soon as they would arrive. They understood.

At Spider Rapids where Roger and Dorothy Nordaas worked, we had a special program to dedicate new Baniwa New Testaments. Dorothy prepared some drawings on construction paper showing how the Christians had received the Word of God in their language many years ago. They were greatly impressed that others had been persecuted for their faith in the Lord Jesus. Then each one of the elders received a copy of the revised New Testament in his language.

Giving out the Baniwa New Testament.

As we left each village the Indians stood near the edge of the river, mothers with little babies on their hips, fathers with their boys nearby. Some were waving their hands, others stood with their arms crossed. Would we ever see each other again here on earth?

CHAPTER THIRTY-FOUR

NEW DOOR OPENS

During the years we were working in Manaus in the mission office, we were able to make yearly trips to visit the churches on the Isana River. In 1979 my father had another stroke and was hospitalized. We were called to go home and spend some time with him before he would go to his Maker. So, in the beginning of August we went to Canada to be at his bedside. Within two weeks he passed on. The funeral was a time of celebration of a life well lived. During the last number of years he was on the board of directors of New Tribes Mission of Canada. He enjoyed that position very much and felt God was using him.

I remember the day when we got a phone call from my father. He had had a stroke but was able to talk. I noticed that he was very weepy. Before he gave the phone to my sister I told him, "Dad, I want to tell you something. Listen carefully. I want you to know I love you very much and am proud you are my father." Thereupon he began weeping and gave the phone to my sister.

My parents had come to visit us in Manaus in 1966 when Luanne was a baby. Dad really enjoyed himself but Mother couldn't take the constant heat. They had left Canada in winter and arrived in the Amazon area of Brazil during its hottest season. It was just too much for her. She never came back to see us, although Dad came two more times. One time he came with Audrey, our oldest daughter, after she graduated from nursing school. Two years later he accompanied Joanne, our second daughter. Dad enjoyed himself very much each time he came to see us. Then after he had several strokes God took him Home to be with Himself in 1979.

It was hard for Mother after Dad passed away. She deteriorated progressively, was completely bedridden and was unable to communicate. She passed away in December of 1984. We were unable to attend the funeral. We had just been at NTM's headquarters in Sanford, Florida to help print the revised Baniwa New Testament and were back in Brazil.

Then in June of 1985 we returned to Canada in poor health and quite discouraged. Slowly health returned and we wondered what God had in store for us. We wanted to be involved in God's work. It wasn't long before

He sent the answer right into our home. The brother of our coworker was in our town speaking in a church. He dropped in to see us.

We had met Warren Bathke in Brazil when he was there to visit his sister Hazel. He enquired about the Indian work where we, and his sister, had worked. After hearing our story and the need for somebody to teach the Baniwas he asked us, "Have you ever thought about teaching them by radio?"

"Well, no," Edna and I replied, almost in unison.

Warren presented the possibility of a radio ministry. After much discussion, he left us, greatly encouraged. It was the beginning of a very meaningful ministry by radio. But, we still didn't have any definite direction as to how to go about it.

Some months later Hazel Bathke came to visit us with two of her sisters and brother-in-law. They were on their way west to see the Canadian Rockies in their motor home. We had a great time reminiscing about times together in the work. After a few days they were on the road again.

One evening in a roadside campground they met another couple also preparing to stay overnight. This second couple, Edmund and Marly Spieker, who were Brazilians, were traveling east. They had been studying the English language and were on the way to Trans World Radio headquarters in New Jersey, U.S.A. They saw this motor home with a church bumper sticker on it and went over to talk to them. In the course of conversation they discovered that they all knew us. As soon as the Spiekers arrived at Edna's niece's place they called us to come and see them. They were overjoyed to be able to speak Portuguese again after a long time away from their own country. We talked to them about teaching our Baniwa believers over the radio. They, of course, were very enthusiastic about it since they worked with Trans World Radio.

CHAPTER THIRTY-FIVE

RADIO MINISTRY

Soon we were in pursuit of a radio ministry to the people we had worked with. Everyone we talked to thought it was an excellent venture. The pastors and the missions committee of our church encouraged us very much. They all promised to pray with us about this change of direction in our ministry.

The burden for the Baniwas continued to be heavy on our hearts. We prayed much and discussed this with concerned people. The suggestion that we teach the Indians by radio sounded far-fetched, but we looked into this possibility. Soon the way opened up to us. God provided us with sufficient money to begin the programs through the generous offering of our church's Sunday School Christmas program.

Mission leaders were approached and they approved it as well and signed a contract with Trans World Radio to broadcast one fifteen minute program every Saturday morning.

We were excited about the prospect of talking to our dear Christian friends all over the jungles of northwestern Brazil, parts of Colombia and Venezuela every week.

Trans World Radio wanted a six-month supply of tapes, before they would begin airing them. So, I began preparing Bible lessons on Ephesians and Colossians. After thirty lessons I began using teaching material especially prepared for teaching indigenous people, called *Building on Firm Foundations*, prepared by Trevor McIlwain and published by New Tribes Mission.

These lessons teach the Bible in a chronological way so that people who previously have not had teaching about God would be able to understand and get to know Him. I was sure, right from the beginning, that these lessons would be excellent for the Christian believers as well as for others.

I opened and closed each radio program with a song the Baniwas knew, leaving me fourteen minutes of teaching. Included in the fourteen minutes was a request for them to write and tell me if they were listening.

The day came when the first program was aired and the Baniwas were thrilled to hear my voice and began writing letters to tell me they were listening. Since there was no postal service in the Indian villages it took their small folded, glued shut letters many months to arrive here. They gave their letters to the missionaries of the area who then mailed them to us, sometimes up to thirty in a package.

We were excited when the first letter arrived from an Indian telling us about the programs. Getulio's parents had become Christians when he was a young boy studying at the religious mission boarding school. After he came home he also accepted Jesus as his Savior but he struggled with worldly temptations for many years. After he finally had victory, he grew in the faith and became a strong leader in the church. He wrote the following letter:

February 5, 1988

My friend Mr. Henry Loewen,

I'm writing a short letter to you, I your friend Getulio. You wanted us to write to let you know that we hear your early morning messages. Yes, we hear them in our own Baniwa language.

We are very glad to hear the messages. We heard them at our conference, at Vista Alegre. We were about 250 people together listening to them with joy. We all want you to keep on speaking to us. I know our Father God is giving you wisdom to work for us and remember us from a far distance. We thank God for you whenever we pray to Him.

Now I want to add something so you'll know how we are doing in God. I notice we are becoming stronger and remain more steadfast in God's Word. Seven villages get together to study, which works out very well for us. Some of the leaders are becoming stronger in God. The young men join with the older men which makes us all very happy.

Your friend,

Getulio Aureliano da Silva

Another listener wrote:
"Now we have our own radio program. It belongs to us."

Edna and I carefully read each letter so that we would get the message they were sending. Some of them would omit words leaving us to guess what they were saying. Others scribbled so badly, we had to go over them again and again to get the meaning. However, most of them were easy to read and we praised God for them.

An old Christian woman had her grandson write a letter telling me she was listening to me talk on the radio and was so happy when she heard my voice but was very sad at the same time because she couldn't see my face.

More letters arrived from listeners in Brazil, many from Columbia and some from Venezuela.

"I felt like crying when I first heard you speak on the radio. I also believe."

"My heart and soul are happy to hear you teach."

"We love to hear you tell us God's Word."

"My heart is happy to know you remember us."

"I'm happy to hear you speak God's Word. Keep on speaking to us."

"I'm happy to hear you explain God's Word in our language."

"I want you to keep on speaking to us. We love it."

"We're glad to hear you teach us about God's Word. We want more."

"I listen to you together with those in my care."

"We want more messages from you."

"Don't stop teaching us."

"We believe what you're teaching us."

A bedridden man from another tribe who understands Baniwa wrote to tell me that he always tuned in to hear me teach in Baniwa and had his whole family sit and listen while he interpreted it for their benefit.

One letter came from a village called Canada. It was named, by the Indians, after our homeland. The letter said they had bought a radio with large speakers and turned it on high volume so everyone in the village could hear the messages.

Some wrote they used their radio cassette players to record the message then played it over again and again and so many others heard the message.

Another Curipaco brother wrote:

"I'm writing to you, our friend Pastor Henry. We're always waiting to hear you teach us each Saturday morning. So, we want you to always teach us the Word for we gladly wait to hear your teaching, here on the radio.

Please keep on teaching us every Saturday, do not ever stop teaching us until our Lord Jesus returns.

I want to tell you about our elders who watch over us. Our enemy wants to deceive them; therefore pray for them and for all of us too, for our enemy the devil walks about powerfully trying to deceive us.

I want you to pray for us that we will remain firm when our evil enemy the devil tempts us.

Then I want you to send me a letter so I will know you joyfully remember those you teach via radio.

That is all I have to say to you our friend Pastor Henry."

Adilson Lino Gomes

Sophie Muller was spending time in Venezuela because her life was in danger in Columbia. She rarely went into Columbia for that reason. However, she went at one time, to attend one of the Bible conferences, in a large village near an airstrip. While she was there with the people she loved, it rained very much and the airstrip became very soggy so the plane was unable to land. She asked the Indians to take her back in the canoe with a motor. Then after she had arrived she was informed there were guerrilla men on the plane who had planned to abduct her. How she praised God for saving her by sending much rain.

At another conference in an Indian village she was awakened early in the morning when it was still dark, by a radio with the volume on high. She thought it was much too loud, and the Indians were supposed to get their sleep so they could sit through the meetings the next day.

When she went to tell them to turn off the radio, she heard it was my radio program they had tuned in and wanted everybody to be able to hear it. She meekly turned around to go to her hammock praising God for the teaching of His Word.

Another Curipaco brother gave the following letter to Sophie Muller, in Venezuela.

"I write this paper to you Pastor Henry, I, your friend Chief Alexander from Sunset Village on the Brazilian border. Our hearts are happy when we hear your speak here about the Word of God on the radio. We want you to speak to us some more, tell us everything about God's Word and about the world too. We want you to know that we want to hear you more because we too trust in God's Word like you teach us.

Many greetings to you and I want you to pray to God for me."

Jesus said "I will build my church". His church is under construction among the Baniwa people and others who hear His Word. He will build it until He comes to gather His own.

One dear saint wrote to us, *"whenever I hear you teach I feel so close to Jesus."*

Our hearts rejoiced when we read *"do not ever stop teaching us until our Lord Jesus returns."*

In gratitude to the Author and Finisher of our faith Edna and I say, "Oh God, you have done for us exceeding abundantly above what we could have asked or thought. Nothing compares with how your Word worked in the hearts of these people in the rainforest."

Henry R. Loewen

POSTSCRIPT

In spite of the difficulties our children had to go through because of our ministry among tribal people they developed into wonderful, dedicated people.

Of course it was hard for them to be separated from parents during the school years, but they understood. They knew it was their part of our ministry. Maybe it was because of this each one of them became valuable citizens and blessings.

Audrey, our oldest daughter, became a good Registered Nurse. She married Fred Otto whom she met in the missionary training school. They went to Brazil and worked in a primitive tribe for several years. Later they began their ministry in the Missionary Training Institute in Brazil. They have a son and daughter.

Joanne, our second daughter, also became an RN. Later she took missionary training and returned to Brazil. There she did linguistic work in one tribe and after that taught linguistics to missionary candidates in Brazil. She married Paul (Buck) Nageli, in Brazil. They have a son and daughter. After some years she taught in the mission's boarding school.

Arlene, also became an RN and practiced in Canada ever since. She married Wayne Kroeker, has two daughters, both married. She worked most of the time in the local hospital's emergency ward. She is very active in her church and has a very tender heart towards needy people.

Jim, our son, took aviation training in Canada after he finished high school in Brazil. His ambition, ever since a young lad, was to be a pilot. He earned a degree in aviation at Trinity Western University. He married Becky Curtis, a former student in the same school in Brazil. He served in Bolivia for more than 18 years. They have two sons.

Luanne, our youngest, did not have the privilege of growing up in a tribal area, by then we had been reassigned to work at mission headquarters in the city of Manaus. After finishing high school in Brazil she attended Bible College and earned a degree. While there she met Brent Toderash and they were married. A few years later she took training to become an LPN. She chose that course because she wanted to have close contact with sick people. This has been her ministry. She is very active in her church. They have two daughters.

ABOUT THE AUTHOR

Henry Loewen gave himself to learning the Baniua language "from scratch" as he and his family lived along the Isana River in northwestern Brazil. Eventually his translation of the complete New Testament became the first complete New Testament ever printed in an Indian language in Brazil. But oh! The trials along the way.

Enemies of the Gospel added to the difficulties of Nature along their rocky waterway. But God was on the side of the missionaries.

Today, radio has carried on the message of the printed page. Indians who understand Baniwa are carrying on the messages also. Jean Dye Johnson - Author of several books

* * * * * *

"The full impact of Henry Loewen's life will only be fully revealed in Heaven. Tribal people in the Northwest section of Brazil are reading and writing in their own language. They are also reading the Baniua New Testament, translated by Henry, and the Nyengatu New Testament started by him. Bible study lessons prepared by Henry are being broadcast on two different radio stations being heard in that part of Brazil, also in Colombia and Venezuela. He has prepared the same lessons in printed forms. They are also going out to the listeners. Thanks to Henry, and his wife Edna, for their leader abilities and consecrated dedication to the task There are even now, and will be, many more tribal people you will get to meet and know in Heaven. Their work continues." - Jim and Skip Curtis co-workers in the same tribe.

Printed in the United States
25262LVS00003B/76-279